ONE MISSION

LEADERSHIP LESSONS FOR A LIFETIME

TO AFRICA

ONE MISSION

LEADERSHIP LESSONS FOR A LIFETIME

TO AFRICA

Strategies for effective teamwork in multicultural, multinational, multi-agency, and multijurisdictional undertakings.

Dr. Peter VanAmburgh

One Mission to Africa Leadership Lessons for a Lifetime

For more information contact 1Mission Leadership, 880 Marietta Highway, Suite 630-333, Roswell, GA 30075, info@1mleadership.com or visit our website at: www.1mleadership.com.

First Edition April 2015
Editors: Gina VanAmburgh, MA, and Denisia Dunmore, PhD
Front and Back Cover design: Rachel VanAmburgh, Renee VanAmburgh
Author photo: Haigwood Studios
Photos courtesy: Sandra Smith, Tiffany Sneed
Photo Edits and Illustrations: Renee VanAmburgh
ISBN: 978-0-9962151-0-7
Library of Congress Control Number: 2015904970
ISNI: 0000-0001-2797-2633
Printed and bound in the United States of America

Preface

Rarely can you rest the worth of a career's research, experience and lessons in a single operation or mission, but that is exactly what happened in Uganda in 2009. The mission described in this book, Exercise Natural Fire 10, was the largest and most complicated multinational endeavor undertaken by the U.S. Military in East Africa up to that date. In today's world the mission can be characterized as a blueprint for current U.S. and international efforts to fight the spread of the Ebola Virus Disease (EVD) in West Africa.

Natural Fire 10 was one of a host of ongoing security cooperation events designed to create opportunities for collaboration, training, and preparation for contingencies with various allies and other nations. These theater-level events are routinely carried out around the world by each of the U.S.'s unified geographic combatant commands: Africa Command (AFRICOM), Central Command (CENTCOM), European Command (EUCOM), Northern Command (NORTHCOM), Pacific Command (PACOM), and Southern Command (SOUTHCOM). These missions rarely rate significant media attention despite their successes and the value they create for preparing the U.S. and its allies for emergency situations before they erupt. This is the story of one of those proactive successes that should be used as a "how-to" guide for individual, local, regional and international operations.

Natural Fire 10 involved moving people and equipment from around the world into a remote area of Northern Uganda along the

South Sudan border. The U.S. contributed Army, Navy, Air Force, Marine, and civilian personnel who were teamed with military members from Burundi, Kenya, Rwanda, Tanzania and Uganda for a coalition effort. While planning took place beforehand, no one on the ground in the tactical component had previously worked together or rehearsed the mission collectively. Some of the leader tests necessary to pull off this tremendous mission included overcoming language barriers, cultural biases, space, constrained time, crises responses, the threat of terrorist attacks, laws and jurisdictional issues, organization, and logistics.

Despite the challenges, the diverse partners were united in their desire to complete the mission. The results produced from this ad hoc group were impressive: 11,698 local Ugandans treated for medical and dental issues, two schools and a medical clinic rebuilt, African partners trained, no security issues, no local law violations, no nongovernmental organizational (NGO) or faith-based organizational activities interrupted, the safe withdrawal and return of all U.S. and African country personnel and equipment, and a tremendous sense of accomplishment and unity by the men and women who participated and supported the mission.

The complex environment of Natural Fire 10 provided a perfect backdrop to explore leadership lessons from a theory, application, and implication approach. Leaders in business, government, NGO, faith-based organizations, and the military can learn from this mission and use the lessons as a guide during future local or international endeavors. After 28 years of demanding leadership roles around the world with the U.S. Army, this mission was unique. It presented all the variables, risks, tests, and successes to serve as a pinnacle experience of applied leadership. I believe by grasping the information shared in this book, readers will be equipped to make sound leadership, organizational, and human-factor decisions.

Acknowledgements

There are many that deserve acknowledgement in this endeavor but God is first – the results of Natural Fire 10, and any successes I have experienced along the way, have been along the path that He has chosen. Thank you. To the members of the Special Operations Forces and Intelligence communities with whom I shared hardships, I owe you all a debt of gratitude that cannot be expressed in words. To the Soldiers, Sailors, Airmen, and Marines of the U.S., Burundi, Kenya, Rwanda, Tanzania and Uganda who performed this mission, you represented the best of each country and it was an honor to serve with you.

A special thank you to the following people who directly contributed their leadership insights, stories and pictures to this endeavor. Without your keen eye for detail and extraordinary wisdom this book would not have been possible:

George Allen	Sandra Smith
Raquel Durden	Tiffany Sneed
Chris Marshall	Lisa Souders
Leif Rivera	Scott Turner
Lance Rygmyr	Alberto Willecke
Bruce Scullion	Carl Welsh

Lastly to my wife Gina, and daughters Renee and Rachel, thank you for always supporting my service no matter where it took me or what risks it entailed. This book would not have been possible without your encouragement, accountability, focus, transcription, edits, artistic input, and enduring love.

Table of Contents

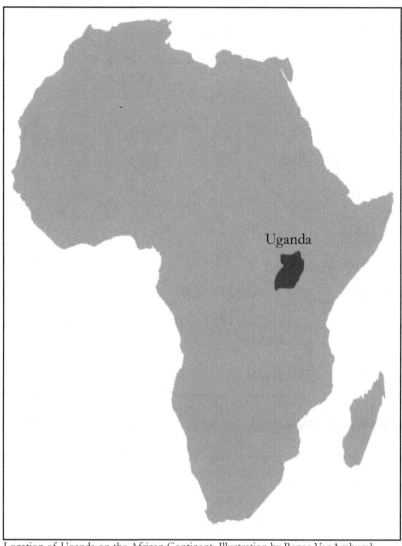

Location of Uganda on the African Continent. Illustration by Renee VanAmburgh.

Map of Uganda. The staging area for Natural Fire 10 would be in Entebbe while the tactical operations of Task Force Kitgum would be located near Kitgum. Illustration by Renee VanAmburgh.

Introduction

The main reason I wrote this book was because this story needed to be told. There is rarely appropriate media visibility of government-sponsored events (particularly military related actions) which had a positive impact on the participants and the community. Natural Fire 10 represents one of many unpublicized operations around the world that not only had a positive effect on the participants and community, but also provided a blueprint for future humanitarian operations in Africa.

Secondly, this book was written to share valuable leadership lessons with several audiences. The first audience is the relatively new leader who seeks to understand the fundamentals of leadership and how to apply those concepts from a practitioner perspective. The Natural Fire 10 mission in Africa provided a compelling true story to illustrate the implications and value of applied leadership. The next audience are governmental, non-governmental or faith-based leaders who are currently preparing for, or in the process of, building a team from disparate groups or organizations. The lessons contained in this book will assist leaders in developing strategies for serving in multinational, multi-agency, multijurisdictional and multicultural organizations. The third audience is the leader who wants a playbook for preparing and executing operations in complex and challenging environments. There are enduring leadership lessons with the validity to reproduce similar outcomes. It is very possible to replicate or reconstruct aspects of Natural Fire 10 and expect similar positive results in Africa and other countries in the world. Finally, the last audience are those people interested in learning and want to be entertained by something meaningful. What you will find in these pages is a compelling story that is both positive and true.

I have organized this book to follow the general chronology of the Natural Fire 10 operation. There are five sections, each with specific chapters that are segmented to divide important parts of the mission. The early chapters follow the logical progression of the story from mission assignment through each step then concluding with redeployment. As the mission unfolds through each chapter, so in turn do the leadership concepts in a way that builds upon previous material. The writing is designed to immerse the reader into a situation, provide understanding, and articulate an important lesson.

Each chapter begins with a contextual story that captures the essence of a key lesson. The remaining pages seek to provide understanding of that story and lessons from a leadership and organizational perspective. The Epliogue in Section Four of the book serves as a summary illustration of the concepts contained herein. Upon reading this book in its entirety, it is hoped that individuals will not only have a sense of what occurred during Natural Fire 10, but also understand why things worked in a way that achieved such a desirable result.

Considerable work went into developing and presenting this material in a way that would be as easily understood to first-line supervisors as to strategic leaders in an organization. Additionally, the lessons have a certain "universality," that should transcend organizational hierarchy and cultural divides. Adhering to the guidelines identified in this book should allow leaders to develop situation-specific strategies to successfully influence multinational, multicultural, multi-agency and multijurisdictional operations in the United States and abroad. Even if a person is not preparing or leading any mission, at least he or she can gain a greater understanding of the complexities of leadership. Finally, the Appendix is purposed to provide a summary and quick reference guide for the leadership strategies and key lessons from this book.

PROLOGUE

Crisis at Palabek Kal

It was early morning October 18, 2009 and the sun was already starting to heat the Task Force Kitgum headquarters. The headquarters was configured as a tactical operations center (TOC) located in a large 100' x 40' white canvass tent that housed the personnel and communications gear to support Task Force operations. The TOC was austere and somewhat cramped yet designed in a functional manner to support the mission. For the majority of the 1,009 members of this coalition effort, the daily regimen of physical training, personal hygiene, and breakfast was complete. The soldiers, sailors, airmen and marines of the six participating countries prepared for the various activities for the day. These missions included security, medical operations, construction, training, logistics support, and management of the Task Force's business.

The coordinating staff was busy preparing for the 9:00 a.m. commander's update briefing. This presentation provided a daily overview of the Task Force elements. In addition to general operational information and synopsis of the upcoming 72 hours, today's brief would provide specific attention to the day's main effort - the medical operation at the Palabek Kal Township's medical health clinic. Palabek Kal was purposed to test the Task Force's ability to project its security force forward and conduct one of many humanitarian assistance missions scheduled for the days ahead. It was a clear day, the timelines were being adhered to, and everything was going according to plan.

Figure P.1. Marines prepare the convoy for departure to Palabek Kal. It would be a good day for testing our Task Force procedures, communications, and leadership. Photo by Author.

Earlier that morning at approximately 7:30 a.m., 95 Task Force members of the Palabek Kal operation assembled about one kilometer from the TOC for a convoy and mission brief. The talented team included 47 U.S. personnel and 48 soldiers assigned from Burundi, Kenya, Rwanda, Tanzania and Uganda. The scene was a jumble of uniforms. The U.S. Marines were decorated in their desert digital camouflage pattern, the U.S. Air Force personnel arrayed in flight suits, medical scrubs and their tiger-striped uniforms, U.S. Army Civil Affairs (CA) and Psychological Operations (PSYOPs) personnel were in civilian attire, other U.S. Army Soldiers in their digital camouflage, and the East Africans in a variety of green camouflage patterns and olive green gear. The contrasting patterns and uniforms were a great visual representation of the joint and multinational effort readying to help the people in the Palabek Kal Township.

The group was crowded in a circle around a team of U.S. Marines who were explaining the mission and convoy brief. The personnel listened intently as a Marine sergeant discussed call signs, checkpoints, actions if the convoy were attacked, actions if a vehicle breaks down, and a host of other contingencies. This was serious business and taken seriously by all those involved. The entire region had been engulfed in a bloody insurgency perpetrated by Joseph Kony and his Lord's Resistance Army (LRA) over the previous 10 years and the threat to the Task Force was real. This first outreach event would be a lucrative target to derail the coalition effort in this region and therefore no chances were being taken with the protection of the force. I positioned myself in the rear of the crowd to support the Marines explaining the briefing and to ensure that all safety and security procedures were being adhered to.

Following the briefing from the Marine sergeant, the Palabek Kal team took to their vehicles. There were 12 Marines in the role of the main U.S. security element complimented by 25 African soldiers comprising the East African security force. Also in the mix, were five CA personnel from different U.S. military services, three Army PSYOPs Soldiers, and a combination of 50 medical personnel from the U.S. and the African partners. The Marines mounted into their High Mobility Multi-Wheeled Vehicles (HMMWVs), commonly pronounced HUMVEEs. These desert tan vehicles were in the typical U.S. Marine military police configuration with turret and light machine guns mounted on the top. The medical personnel were loaded into several busses, the CA and PSYOPs Soldiers took to safari-looking civilian vehicles, and the African security personnel climbed into an interesting array of military trucks. I looked on as this assortment of military and civilian vehicles departed out of the basecamp and down an unimproved red clay road. My first thought was "This will be a great day of learning for all of us."

The trek over rough and dusty roads took approximately forty-five minutes. The lead vehicles had it easy compared to the remainder of the convoy engulfed in a cloud of red dust. Nonetheless, the passengers looked intently for any signs of trouble while taking in the landscape. The area was relatively open plains with tall grass intermixed with dense scrub vegetation. Sporadic groves of trees were the main source of shade and protection from the sun. The living conditions were sparse. The region's Acholi tribes were once peasant farmers thriving on maize and long horned cattle. They lived in small villages scattered across the countryside in round clay huts with thatch roofs called Bantu huts. Normally built with a double layer of bamboo, palms or wood covered with clay

Figure P.2. Typical Bantu hut in the Kitgum area. Photo by Tiffany Sneed.

and roofed with grass or banana thatch, these small huts dotted the landscape. Unfortunately, 20 years of war made a significant impact on the Acholi and many of the small villages and homes were abandoned for dusty encampments along major roads and on the outskirts of towns. These camps provided safety from marauding bands of LRA fighting against the Ugandan People's Defense Force (UPDF). The Bantu huts in the camps were crowded together with very little area for farming and were host to a plethora of free roaming animals including scrawny looking chickens, goats and an occasional cow soaking up the relentless sun.

As the convoy made its way along the main road from Kitgum to Palabek Kal, young people in brightly covered clothes would emerge from their small Bantu homes. We would find that war and disease had relegated many families to be headed by children who would look on with both interest and suspicion of the military presence. Despite the Ugandan government's campaign to rid the region of murderous LRA insurgents, their reign of terror and the UPDF's heavy hand at combatting them still traumatized the locals. In most cases, fear and distrust of anyone armed was the normal reaction by the local population. This was a tremendous challenge for Task Force Kitgum and at every opportunity the team's coalition elements worked to overcome those local perceptions by friendly gestures, minimizing aggressive posture and weapons visibility, and ensuring first contact was with Ugandan or East African personnel.

As previously instructed, the U.S. personnel in the convoy communicated their friendly intentions by smiling and waving at every opportunity. Earlier I had given guidance to many in the Task Force to "Smile and wave - every chance you get. This may be the only time these people will see an American service person so be positive." Throughout the operation we would find that a positive attitude and engagement went a long way in reducing anxiety and signifying our friendly intent to this reserved population. The children were always the first to respond to us and their reaction would permeate to the adults who generously participated by always returning a smile and a wave.

As the convoy neared Palebak Kal's medical clinic, the passengers could see the township emerge. The groupings of Bantu huts became more prevalent and gave way to several walled buildings that were painted red with metal roofs. Coinciding with the increase in dwellings, the road opened from a single lane into a wider roadway but still comprised of red dirt and clay. The anticipation of the mission gripped some on the convoy while others were just looking forward to getting out of the vehicles and the dust. The Marines increased their vigilance as the township came into view. As the convoy negotiated its way into the center of the small town, a collective apprehension fell over the Task Force personnel. Tremendous crowds were on the street.

For the Marines and East Africans charged with providing security for the event large crowds equated to a potential threat. To the medical personnel, masses meant an overwhelming amount of work. For the CA personnel the large gathering was a great showing of support for the effort, and for the PSYOPs team this multitude of people was an opportunity to test the messages and gain understanding of local communications. It was clear to the group that all the training received and preparation was about to be put to the test.

The convoy drove on toward the medical facility entrance. As they arrived at the gate, they were overwhelmed to see thousands of people already lined up, waiting for the opportunity to see a doctor. For some of the local Ugandans in the crowds, mainly of the Acholi tribe, this event would be the first time that many would have access to modern medical care. Men, women and children were patiently waiting in a long line that stretched for over a mile. There were people with crutches, some had the posture of being in pain with an obvious ailment, entire families and others stood in line with conditions not yet diagnosed or treated.

Although we expected and planned for large numbers of people at the Palabek Kal clinic, it was a challenge for the medical planners to anticipate the capacity of need in the area. The CA team had visited the location several times prior for coordination with the local administrators and found not only a local care requirement but potentially an international need as well. With the Palabek Kal Township only a few kilometers from the South Sudan border, there was a chance that a flood of refugees would move south for medical care. Many of the Task Force personnel in the convoy noted during the drive to Palebak Kal that they passed plenty of people along the route apparently heading in the direction of the clinic. It was concluded that the current crowd, like the temperature was likely to increase as the day went on. Many of the medical experts inferred that a growing crowd, increasing temperatures, little to no shade, and a capacity limitation of about 1,000 patients per day looked like a "long day" indeed.

The lead U.S. Marine vehicle made its way to the first barricade tied in with a ring of concertina wire that served as the external perimeter around the medical clinic. The barricade was moved by UPDF forces whom had been on site for the previous four days to ensure that the Task Force element would not encounter an ambush or bombing by the LRA. After positioning the vehicles in a defensive posture, the Marine military police and African security force quickly moved in through the external ring of concertina wire to the internal gate manned by Ugandan military personnel. The gate was part of an old nine-foot chain link fence that surrounded the clinic and would serve as the internal safe zone.

Figure P.3. Gate at a medical health center. Notice the police, African security force, and the Marine on the far left, representing the three rings of security at the clinic. Photo by Sandra Smith.

The clinic's security perimeter was essentially a series of concentric rings covered by approximately 70 armed personnel. The outer band was manned by the local police force dressed in khaki uniforms and carrying batons and handguns. The next layer of defense was comprised of UPDF soldiers under the direct authority of the Task Force Kitgum Deputy Commander. The Ugandans were armed with a modern variant of the Russian AK-47 (AKM) and were very familiar with the regions population and threats. Inside the UPDF ring the coalition's African soldiers were arrayed in a circle around the clinic also armed mostly with AKMs excluding the Kenyan soldiers who carried a version of the German G3 assault rifle. The last line of defense was the U.S. Marine element carrying M9 pistols, M16 rifles and M240 Squad Automatic Weapons (SAWs). The Marines were the final option to protect the medical team if the threats or potentially hostile crowds were to overwhelm the local police, UPDF and East African coalition force outside the clinic fence line. The concentric security rings ensured a coalition goal was achieved to have an "African face" or lead throughout the operation. By positioning the Ugandan's on the periphery, then East African's and finally posting the Ma-

7

Figure P.4. African security forces offload vehicle. Photo by Author.

rine elements in the center or the innermost ring of the perimeter, local inhabitants would first see and interface with local and regional African forces.

The Marines and East African security contingent went to work immediately fanning out into their prescribed positions to protect the health professionals and the facility from potential threats. Inside the clinic's boundaries the Task Force medical team assigned to this event, a group of U.S. Army and Air Force medical professionals with a smaller group of East African counterparts, began to set up their operation alongside the local clinic's indigenous personnel. The facility was constructed of several old cinder block and cement buildings with metal roofs, dirt floors, no electricity, and limited running water. Fortunately, the Task Force brought modern facilities with them and went to work setting up a hasty renovation including electrical generators and purified water sources. The Task Force's African counterparts were very much part of the medical team effort; however, the modern equipment provided by the U.S. relegated their work to a support role. They began cleaning the rooms and preparing all the equipment for performing minor medical and dental procedures. It was a marvel to see a crude facility transformed into a modern care unit in a span of hours. Throughout the preparation inside the perimeter, the U.S. Marine security element did their best to balance relationship building with security. Their presence and demeanor clearly displayed that they were a professionally trained and equipped force not to be reckoned with.

The UPDF and East African partners erected a tent just inside the final internal security point, to serve as the triage center.

Figure P.5. UPDF Medical Officer speaking in Acholi addresses locals in the triage tent. Photo by Sandra Smith.

Triage is the process of determining a patient's treatment based on need and resources. Traige centers are normally associated a with a crisis or emergency dealing with a large population of victims. The casualties must be allocated limited resources based on a system of priorities. Part of the coalition training was employing a triage approach at Palabek Kal and other clinics to effectively deal with the large crowds expected at each event. The triage center was one of the key interfaces with the local patients. Much like the security component, the medical activities had to have an "African face" and the UPDF provided the primary personnel for operating this important process.

The triage tent accommodated approximately 40 people with seating in folding chairs and served as a control point to manage the care. Once patients entered the triage, the team separated medical issues from dental, and acute from chronic conditions. As people were moved from the triage tent to open treatment rooms, others outside the security perimeter were now allowed into the clinic to fill those seats and await their opportunity for care. The triage center staff managed the caseload, a constant source of medical preventative education delivered by a female Ugandan military lieutenant in the local

Acholi language to those awaiting treatment.

One of the main goals of Natural Fire 10 was to increase the ability of the host nation (Uganda) and east African partners to respond to widespread medical emergencies. The original expectation was that the coalition medical professionals would work side-by-side while simultaneously providing diagnosis and care to the local patients. As they began working together, it became readily apparent that the African partner expertise and training was not to the same standard as the U.S. component. Thus, the shared responsibility for treatment transformed into a mentor and protege relationship. The U.S. doctors and dentists essentially supervised and guided the African medical personnel through the treatment protocols and procedures.

The entire clinic coordination and setup took approximately two hours. During that timeframe back at the TOC, another convoy consisting of a Marine security element, an Army military police protective detail and myself were preparing to depart the basecamp. The purpose of this movement to the Palabek Kal health clinic was to observe first-hand the conduct of the mission and if necessary direct the adjustment of resources to support the main effort for the day. After a safety and security briefing that mirrored the earlier convoy, our smaller three-vehicle caravan departed the basecamp's main gate in route to the Palabek Kal Township.

Our group made its way along the identical dusty road to the clinic. We passed alike scenes and an increasing volume of people undoubtedly now moving in the direction of the clinic. Again, every effort to dispel fear of armed military personnel by waving and smiling as the group passed people on the route was balanced with the security of the small three-vehicle convoy. My vehicle seemed to arrive precisely as the first collection of patients were brought into the triage center commencing the operation.

The arrival of the command team signaled to the element leaders at the clinic an opportunity for an update or guidance. I consulted with the Marine sergeant in charge, the CA officer, the PSYOPs team leader, the Air Force medical team leader and found that everything was in order. The elements at Palabek Kal had each worked their respective parts and made necessary adjustments to the plan. These changes were based on conditions and requirements on the ground at the clinic. One issue that had come up from a previous visit by the higher level commander, a 2-star Army general from U.S. Army Africa (USARAF), was to ensure that the U.S. Marines were in a low threat posture and kept their weapon systems out of the eyes of the local population. This was to physically remind all that this mission was peaceful in nature and should not be construed as threatening in any way. With that in mind, I consulted with the Marine Officer in Charge (OIC) and gave the order to have only side arms on the Marine element in direct contact with the populace but to ensure that their rifles were nearby and quickly accessible. Any Marine not in the public eye should have their weapons on them at all times. This edict was not popular with the Marines who felt their reaction times to a hostile threat could be delayed.

I walked the perimeter and spoke to the Marine guards about their role. Specifically emphasizing the importance of balancing security with relationship building to attempt to temper their lack of enthusiasm for keeping their M16s away from the perimeter fence where the crowd was close. I made a final series of leader checks that included verifying with the Marine communications sergeant that the satellite link to the TOC was operational, the medical OIC was satisfied, and the PSYOPS team was engaged. By this time the Army PSYOPs team was outside the clinic's perimeter. They were performing their role interviewing and conversing with the people awaiting treatment along the fenceline. The team was attempting to ensure the Task Force mission objectives were being communicated. I performed a last minute walk-through of the medical facilities where the doctors, dentists, and observed the staffs were all hard at work with their first round of patients. The last thing I noted prior to departing back to the headquarters, was the local clinic manager speaking to the people lined up outside on a loudspeaker. He appeared to be instructing the crowds about the procedures for the day.

Satisfied that the security, medical operations, and communications links at Palabek Kal were in order, my security detail and I departed the clinic to return to the TOC. This was but one of several events for the day. A radio check and confirmation was made between my vehicle and headquarters to inform the battle captain that our element was on the move and returning home. The caravan made an uneventful 45-minute return trip to the Task Force Kitgum basecamp.

The UPDF and Army military policeman manning the basecamp security checkpoint jumped to attention as my vehicle went through the main gate towards a grassy parking area adjacent to the TOC headquarters. Almost immediately upon arrival, briskly out of the TOC came the Task Force Executive Officer, Battle Captain, and U.S. Marine Commanding Officer all carrying the distressed look of bad news. Over the last 45 minutes the situation at the Palabek Kal health clinic had taken a turn for the worse with over 3,000 people turning from a docile group awaiting medical treatment into a potential mob. The Task Forces' first crisis was developing. It certainly would be a good day for learning.

SECTION ONE

Leadership

CHAPTER ONE

Stepping Off

In 2009, I had the great privilege of serving as the commander of the 560th Battlefield Surveillance Brigade (BFSB) stationed at Fort Gillem, GA. In late July we received information regarding an upcoming mission on the continent of Africa. U.S. AFRICOM was readying for a "graduate-level" test of the fledging combatant command's capability in an exercise called "Natural Fire 10." The operation was scheduled to commence in East Africa during late September and into October 2009. Despite its pending commencement in a few months, Natural Fire 10 was missing a command and control organization to oversee the most important elements of the mission. It seemed like a perfect fit, AFRICOM needed a headquarters to command and control the exercise, and we were searching for a new challenge. Our potential role involved deploying a brigade headquarters element to Uganda to oversee the execution of a Task Force conducting simultaneous humanitarian assistance and security missions along Uganda's northern border with South Sudan.

The mission sounded straightforward enough until you understood the thousand-person Task Force would be joint, comprised of U.S. Army, Navy, Air Force and Marine personnel, as well as multinational, including soldiers from Burundi, Kenya, Rwanda, Tanzania, and Uganda. The operation was in an area under the threat of insurgent attack. All the planning sessions had been completed without our unit's participation. There were no existing protocols for creating a joint/multinational headquarters using a BFSB for the lead. None of the key leaders, U.S. or African, had worked together nor would they get a chance to meet until they were on the ground in Kitgum, Uganda. The U.S. troops and equipment would be moving by air, sea and land into Uganda. This mission was a huge test of AFRICOM and USARAF's abilities, there was very little time for training and preparation, and significant command-induced anxiety was in the mix. In addition, the mission would begin in just 60 days.

The 560th BSFB's coordinating staff looked at the set of variables, analyzed the work and the individual tasks with the normal skepticism of senior staffers. Their response was predictable: there was not enough time, we do not have all the equipment, we have not been involved in shaping the plans, there were too many unknowns, and we have never done this before. However, having been involved with a variety of unique endeavors during the previous two years they did have a sense of optimism and confidence that if any organization could pull this off – it was their team.

I viewed Natural Fire 10 as an incredible opportunity for both organizational and personal growth. Where else would the brigade be forced to deploy, operate the headquarters in an unfamiliar environment, develop new employment doctrine for the Army, build a coalition of different countries' military forces, and thanks to the humanitarian aspects of the operation – do some good in a hard hit area of Africa? My decision was let's go for it of course!

As a leader, you probably grasp why I would take a look at all the variables, listen to the staff lay out the obstacles to success in this endeavor, yet decide to accept the tremendous personal and professional risks for a mission such as Natural Fire 10. This chapter is devoted to that most intangible element in organizations that seems to transcend resources, facilities, hardships, and the environment but it provides tangible results. It is the subject of historic literature, philosophy, movies, and popular books, and is learned through a complex set of education and experience – and that is leadership.

In this section you will gain an appreciation for the significance of a leader's influence on an organization and its members.

16

The reading will also provide a context from which to view leadership in order to create a transformational environment. Finally the section illustrates behaviors leaders should exhibit, research and literature you should know, application of the theoretical in complex situations, and the results that can be expected. Let's get started.

Leader

Ponder this simple question - what is the meaning of the word "*leader?*" Where does the word come from, what is the origin, and what does it truly represent? If I were in a room full of people and randomly began selecting members of the audience to answer the question, I presume I would hear who leaders *are* - good communicators, smart, self confident... What they *possess* - integrity, charisma, intellect, wisdom, judgment, energy... What they *do* - role model, guide, influence, provide vision, organize, and motivate... and *How* they do it - enlist cooperation, use incentives and influence, develop paths & goals. The responses we would find in our group would be exactly what researchers have discerned over time including lists of traits, behaviors, activities, and processes. It would be a great exercise but it would not answer the question. What does the word *leader* really denote?

Most definitions of the term involve a process of influence that enables the accomplishment of an objective. Essentially leaders influence people to achieve goals. While the influencing nature of leadership is important it does not demonstrate what a leader "*is.*" From an etymological perspective, the word leader is derived from the old English/old Frissian word "leda" or "leadan," meaning the first person who *steps off* in the dance (C. Onions (Ed.), 1966).

What happens when one person steps forward? Others follow. Most people can remember an experience when you had to make that first step and not surprisingly, were followed by others. Words have meaning and understanding what a leader *is*, helps put all the other descriptive elements, traits, behaviors, actions, and processes into context. Hold onto the thought of *stepping off* as we continue.

Allow me to recall my first military free-fall parachute jump. There I was, 19 years old, a Private First Class and had been in the Army for a little over a year. By some huge set of circumstances that were completely incomprehensible to my fellow High Altitude Low Opening (HALO) course members, all sergeants and officers, here I stood, first on the tail ramp of a C-130 Hercules military aircraft. I was the youngest member of the class, and had never made a free-fall parachute jump. Keep in mind the military doesn't have a process for gradually increasing your free fall delays to give you confidence like they do in civilian skydiving certification. Instead, you jump out of an aircraft at 10,000 feet above ground and free-fall 7,000 feet before deploying your parachute. So there I was placed, first in line, with a planeload of senior people at my back.

Take a moment to remember a time when you took that first step. What were the things that led you to move first into the "free-fall" situation I described? You had to overcome fear, needed self-confidence, had to have a vision (in my case it was that the parachute would open), you understood the mission, and you probably had recognition of your responsibility to the rest of the group because of your role as moving first. So you stepped off, took the leap, accepted the risks, were confident in the outcome, and guess what – the people behind you saw you going off and while they may have possessed similar uncertainties, they were influenced by your action and followed.

On the ramp of an aircraft the only parachutist who often has a clear view, other than the jumpmaster, is the first to leap out of the plane. Everyone in the rear puts their faith in the jumpmaster's and lead jumper to ensure they exit in the right location and at the right time. When you are in the lead, both the view and the assessment of risks are different from those who follow. The parachutists in the rear cannot see over the ramp and truly comprehend your view

18

of the ground, the clouds, and the feel of the rushing air. Instead fellow jumpers are left with a myopic scene made up of the person to their immediate front and the next few steps ahead of them. They only have clarity of the next action while you can see and prepare for several moves in advance. They are willing to follow your lead and assume your clear view provides the ability to judge risks and rewards. They must have faith in your judgment to jump, their personal ability to accomplish the next few tasks, the instrumentality (parachute) to deliver them safely and ultimately complete the mission. While the personnel behind you in the aircraft ramp never fully face the same challenge as you, they also do not have time to take in the entire scene until it is too late, and therefore are reliant on your first step.

Let us briefly journey back to the first HALO jump story. I remember thinking to myself on that C-130 ramp, "Well Airborne, here we go." The jumpmaster gave me the signal and I leapt off the ramp. The winds were tremendous as I was caught in the slipstream of the aircraft. I arched my back into a position practiced over and over again, on a table and in a wind tunnel during the previous two weeks of training. As I came into a stable position I suddenly realized I was not going to freeze up and fail to pull the ripcord thereby releasing my parachute when it was time. I remember seeing one of my HALO instructors effortlessly moving around me but did not see another jumper. I glanced at my altimeter over and over as it spun from 10,000 to 9,000 and below concurrent with the terminal velocity speed of about 122MPH. The altimeter reached 4,000 feet and I looked around to ensure my space was clear. I then purposefully moved my right hand over my ripcord while simultaneously moving my left arm in front of my head to compensate and keep me stable. At 3,000 feet, I pulled my ripcord and deployed my parachute. It opened with a tremendous pop and jerked me into an upright position dangling below the MC-1 parachute. It was awesome and the ultimate *stepping off* experience.

I am confident my first jump experience made me stronger,

but positioning the youngest person in the class was a masterful design to strengthen the resolve of others. It placed pressure on that senior group of officers and noncommissioned officers to go through with their first free-fall. I doubt the instructors understood they were employing vicarious modeling from Bandura's Social Cognitive Theory (building confidence in personal self efficacy by observing someone else do a task). However, they recognized that the youngest in the class leading the jump strengthened the resolve of the group. "If this 19 year old kid wasn't scared to jump, well I'm not going to freeze on the ramp" was the general assumption. The simple action of stepping off first is critical for understanding the behavior of a leader.

While the word leader has a significant diversity of definitions, the word *leadership* is a little more universal. Generally, leadership is defined as a process of influence involving at least one other person and it is for goal attainment (Northouse, 1997). The U.S. Army's definition of leadership *"is providing purpose, direction and motivation in order to accomplish the mission and improve the organization"* (Army Doctrine and Training Publication 6-22, 2012). Whatever definition you choose for leadership, the process will ultimately require the ability to influence someone to do something they may or may not want to accomplish on their own.

The purpose of influence in the leadership process is to produce action by others. Leaders can employ positive influence to provide motivation or negative influence to coerce people to perform. When a leader influences a person to action one thing should be realized: only through the action of others will leaders accomplish goals. One should strive to create an environment where leaders recognize that any success achieved will only be through the people in their charge. Here is one of my favorite analogies of a leader's role in organizational and personal growth:

> An organization is like a bucket of water and the leader is a hand for stirring. When a new leader arrives, he/

20

she puts their hand in the bucket and begins stirring the water and creating momentum. However only when the hand is removed can you assess the leader's effect. If the water keeps churning, the leader likely made a developmental investment in the people to continue and enhance the momentum in the bucket. If the hand is withdrawn from the bucket and the water becomes stagnant, you can bet the actions were all leader-centric and failed to develop the team.

You may have read or heard long leadership philosophies that articulate all sort of behaviors, and expectations designed to assist organizational members to understand what is expected of them. I have found the simpler you make your philosophy, the more likely people will understand and employ it. My leadership philosophy is very short "*A leader's role is to help make other people successful.*" When a leader takes the role of serving others, for the purpose of enabling individuals and teams to achieve their potential, the organization succeeds.

One of our first steps preparing for Natural Fire 10 was to acknowledge our leadership role and influence on the mission. First, we had to be willing to *step off* first at every point in the planning, preparation and execution of the mission. Waiting for someone else to take the lead was not an option for us due to the limited time we had until mission execution. Second, our role in leading the operation required a vision and viewpoint that enabled our organization to set the conditions for the units we would be charged with leading. We had to stay engaged and continuously communicate the mission's value. Third, it would be necessary for us to provide action-oriented influence to the participants in order to initiate and sustain momentum. Both from an organizational and personal standpoint, we had to model the role we expected from others. Last, the mission demanded my personal leadership philosophy be nested through the force. Our job as a headquarters was to set the conditions that enabled other participants to realize their potential for contributing expertise and work to the operation. Our success would only be measured by the achievements of each Soldier, Sailor, Airman and Marine and the foreign military person doing their specific jobs in the Task Force.

CHAPTER TWO

Leadership Theories

By mid-August 2009, the 560th BFSB was in a frenetic planning and preparation period. We had accepted the lead role for the tactical component of Natural Fire 10 and began conducting research and constructing comprehensive staff estimates to prepare for the mission. Part of the analysis was devoted to identifying potential threats to the operation and its participants. These risks included environmental hazards such as Malaria, the Plague, EVD, and about all other potentially dangerous diseases known to mankind. We were also concerned with insects, vipers, and other creatures that had the potential to inflict casualties on our team and the entire Task Force. The weather was yet another hazard that could derail our mission as inclement conditions had the potential to inhibit our ability to maneuver by land or air. The final danger was the opportunity for a terrorist strike due to the area of operations and its significance to the LRA or other groups who may be looking for a target to bring publicity to their cause.

As the 560th BFSB staff developed plans to mitigate the external threats, we simultaneously needed to select the final roster of personnel who would serve as the 560th BFSB forward headquarters in Uganda. This sub-element of the brigade would command and control what was now being referred to as Task Force Kitgum. Kitgum was the largest township in Northern Uganda and our proposed basecamp would be constructed about 10 kilometers outside the city. Our late arrival into the planning sequence of Natural Fire 10 meant our participation would have limitations in the number of personnel who could deploy as part of our headquarters. Ultimately, we were only authorized by AFRICOM to bring 24 members of the brigade to Natural Fire 10. The small number due to previously coordinated host nation agreements, airlift considerations, basecamp housing, transportation, feeding, and pay.

Typically when a brigade-level organization is directed to perform command and control functions for overseas missions such as Natural Fire 10, commanders simply turn to their primary staff to fill the key roles. Choosing the regular team of administration (S1), intelligence (S2), operations (S3), and logistics (S4) functional experts is a logical decision that creates immediate efficiencies. In most cases you can assume the primary staff group has worked together before, knows their respective roles, and understands the work output required. For a commander, it is reassuring to know the people you will be working with, that additional training requirements are likely limited, and the group knows how to perform as a team.

Selecting those that you are comfortable with for a mission can provide for efficiency in work production and relationship building. However, those efficiencies almost guarantee that your organizational depth and experience will be limited to a few, instead of shared by many. Effective organizations are more likely to sacrifice some efficiency to ensure specialized experiences are not resident in only one part of the group. Instead, by expanding participation from across your enterprise, a single mission such as Natural Fire 10 can serve to strengthen the capability of your entire organization through those selected for the operation. As those participants return to their respective assignments after the mission, you would have provided the experience across your enterprise instead of limiting it to a small group of people.

My intent for Task Force Kitgum was to gather a cross-section of talent from amongst the 560th BFSB. This would ensure the opportunity and resulting experience was shared across the organization and not confined to only the headquarters. Exercising my

24

wish meant establishing a new team designed specifically to support Natural Fire 10. Some of the criteria I used to pick the 24 member headquarters included:

- Specific military skills - necessary for the performance of key functions in the headquarters while deployed to Uganda;
- Demeanor - their predisposition for keeping a positive or optimistic view;
- Brigade assignment – to ensure each part of the brigade had a representative who would bring back the experience to their respective element upon completion of the mission;
- Diversity - to ensure we had different perspectives for internal processes and represented the U.S. in Uganda by having a mix of male/female and minority participants in key leadership roles;
- Personal growth - how much the mission would move a participant "out of their comfort zone" by the challenges of the mission and operating environment?; and
- Leadership ability – each would essentially lead elements of the Task Force in specific functional areas.

The 24 people were selected and the process started for assembling the group. We began assimilating the members' competencies, skills, and behaviors into a team capable of performing a highly sensitive mission with international ramifications. In addition to the group dynamics internal to developing our Task Force Kitgum team, we had to influence various players at USARAF and AFRICOM, the National Guard Bureau, and the Georgia Army National Guard. All of these organizations possessed a direct or indirect role in our ability to accomplish the mission.

The value of building a new team, requiring them to work under the duress of time, and forcing them to engage with a large group of people at different echelons of command may have been lost to participants initially. Clearly the cross-sectional approach I chose to select members of Task Force Kitgum was not the 'efficient' method

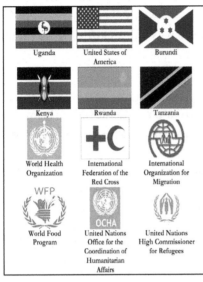

Figure 2.1. The countries and official NGO participants of Natural Fire 10. Illustration by Renee VanAmburgh.

to pick the team. However, the group dynamics and constrained time was the perfect environment to prepare each participant for the leadership challenges our team would assume.

Once in Uganda, our small headquarters staff would have very little time to establish ourselves in the lead and assimilate over a thousand Soldiers, Sailors, Airmen and Marines as well as military members from Burundi, Kenya, Rwanda, Tanzania and Uganda. Then quickly build an organization capable of effectively directing humanitarian, security, and training operations in unfamiliar terrain. Therefore, it was important for each member of the Task Force Kitgum headquarters team to understand leadership, the exercise of direct and indirect influence, group dynamics, and work under significant time and environmental constraints. I needed each of my team members to be an effective leader who could call upon an extensive repertoire of interpersonal and communications abilities to deal with a large and diverse population in a complex organizational context.

When you are confronted with the potential for multicultural, multinational, multi-agency, or multijurisdictional operations, you need to acknowledge one certainty - the greater the diversity of those involved the bigger the challenge to exercise effective leadership. Large, complex and diverse missions require a broad set of leadership competencies. The competencies I am referring to are knowledge, skills and abilities. One truth I have learned about leading is that *more* is better: the *more* you know about leadership, the *more* you

26

develop your skills and behaviors, and the *more* leadership experiences you have, the greater your effectiveness will be as a leader.

Another concept to grasp is that leadership is not a flat endeavor. There is width, depth, height and substance. Leadership is a complex set of interpersonal variables and situational intersections that can result in success or failure at goal attainment. Leadership is both an art and science. Leadership as an art refers to the ability to weave together the right form of influence, at the right time, to the right person resulting in a desired behavior or action. As a science, leadership involves understanding the theoretical frameworks of leadership, building the skills necessary for positive relations and influence, and exhibiting the behaviors associated with successful leaders. The story of Natural Fire 10 involves a successful exercise of applied leadership theory. The following short course can be considered a brief synopsis of the major leadership approaches to provide *more* knowledge about the processes and why they worked.

Leadership Theory Short Course

Generally there are four main theoretical approaches that dominate the research associated with leadership. These approaches represent an evolution of discovery and provide a glimpse into the leadership phenomenon, and each was employed throughout the Natural Fire 10 mission. First are the *trait* theories that focus on what personality characteristics leaders possess. The *behavioral* theories are next with their orientation on what leaders do when leading others. The third approach contains the *contingency or situational* theories that represent the *"how-to"* models and help explain leader actions in different circumstances or situations. Finally, there are the *power and influence* theories that focus on why people behave the way they do during leadership exchanges. In addition to the four leadership approaches, the *transformational leadership* theory provides a unique perspective for study. Understanding leadership theories will provide you greater

Table 2.1

Traits Expected of Leaders

Main Traits Identified for Successful Leaders	Definition
Intelligence	Strong reasoning, verbal ability and perceptual ability provide help to advance ideas in ways for others to grasp.
Self-Confidence	Positive self-esteem and self-assurance instills a belief that something can be accomplished.
Determination	Initiative, drive, persistence, and dominance and the capacity to persevere in the face of obstacles.
Integrity	Honesty, trustworthiness, and adherence to a strong set of principles builds trust.
Sociability	The inclination to seek out social relationships by being friendly, courteous, tactful and diplomatic demonstrates concern for others.

clarity in the complex interplay between leaders and followers.

Trait Approaches

Trait theories are considered some of the earliest attempts to learn what makes a good leader (Bass, 1990). The trait approaches focus on the distinguishing qualities of good leaders. The characteristics, or traits, can be considered personality features possessed by some people but not others. Thanks to the significant volume of trait research, we have an understanding of general traits that appear to characterize a good leader. *Intelligence, self-confidence, determination, integrity* and *sociability* appear to be traits most revered of leaders (Northouse, 1997).

Trait research has evolved significantly over the years. Early trait studies concluded that either an individual had leader characteristics or not. Later research indicated that leadership traits could be learned and developed over time. One important aspect of trait research has been the failure of researchers to link traits to outcomes. In essence, just because a leader appears to possess the desired traits, that alone does not guarantee leader success (Northouse, 1997).

Despite the lack of linkage to outcomes, the vast research on trait theory acknowledges that there are some traits that appear to assist, or are at least expected, of leaders (Northouse, 1997). Table 2.1 depicts the main traits associated with successful leaders. The list is helpful for understanding what characteristics are appealing and expected of leaders from their followers.

The criteria used for selecting the 560th BFSB Natural Fire 10 participants did not overtly address the trait theory. Interestingly, aspects of selection criteria including military skills, demeanor, personal growth and leadership abilities all factored together in a manner that produced a team of people who exhibited the five major traits associated with successful leaders. We would need every possible advantage to lead this mission and recognized that the willingness of Task Force members to follow the 560th BFSB's functional area leaders (S1, S2, S3, S4) would not be solely determined by personal characteristics. However, we understood that certain traits appealed to followers. Therefore we ensured that our team would be filled with those who exhibited the characteristics of successful leaders.

Behavioral Approaches

While traits were one area of importance among the 560th BFSB leadership team selection, leadership behavior was another factor that would be important for the mission. The *behavioral approaches* to leadership theory are based on observable actions that help to explain what leaders *do*. These theories represent a shift from the personality characteristics of the trait theories to the activity of leaders. The two mainstays of the behavioral approaches, style theory and skills theory, represent specific behavior-based frameworks necessary for effective leadership.

Table 2.2

Leadership Styles

Style of Leadership	Description	Strengths	Weaknesses
Authoritative	Leader makes decisions and directs activity. Input from employees is limited. Is optimized when projects or situations require leadership in order to accomplish things quickly.	Works best when time is constrained and decisions are required without time for agreement.	Does not engender support from employees. Can create paralysis in organizational decision-making through micromanaging.
Participative	Leader allows others to contribute to the decision making process. Members provide input and ideas but the leader makes the decision.	Creativity is encouraged and rewarded and employees typically feel more valued.	Does not work well with inexperienced employees. Leader can become more focused on promulgating goodwill instead of accomplishing goals.
Delegative	Relatively hands-off approach. The leader provides little direction and allows members to have freedom to make decisions.	Experienced, motivated and skilled employees benefit by working on their own.	Groups often do not have the maturity to settle disagreements. The ability to manage deadlines and projects can suffer.

Initially, researchers identified three styles of leadership that appeared to characterize the behavior of a leader. These three styles, *authoritarian, participative* and *delegative,* were a starting point for other studies that expanded the understanding and advocated adding leader skill dimensions identified in the leadership processes. The skills dimensions included technical work abilities, human or "people" skills, and conceptual skills that enabled one to see the interconnectivity and application of ideas for problem solving.

Further research into leadership behaviors identified spe-

30

cific dimensions that appeared to explain leadership styles (Blake & Mouton, 1985). One of the most used models from the behavioral approach is the Managerial Grid (Northouse, 1997). The Managerial Grid is based on Blake and Mouton's (1985) identification of two behavioral dimensions: concern for people and concern for production. They constructed a simple grid to characterize leadership styles based on a person-versus-production focus. Both approaches acknowledged that leaders should have a repertoire of leader behaviors and skills that can be applied based on tasks being completed and developmental needs of the people. For the purposes of developing generalizable leader strategies, you should be familiar with the following three styles of leadership as identified in Table 2.2

The value of understanding the behavioral approaches lies within the simplicity of use. The leaders of 560th BFSB had to plan and prepare for the diverse and decentralized operations within the Natural Fire 10 mission and would need to be capable of effortlessly changing their leadership style to the requirements. The behavioral approaches are frameworks for positioning yourself to effectively deal with certain tasks and people requirements.

Contingency/Situational Approaches

Building on the *style* and *skills* approaches, *contingency/situational* theories of leadership are based on the realization that there is no one framework that can guarantee leader success. Instead, leaders should employ the best *style* to achieve results *contingent* on the *situational* or human variables involved. Probably the most popular of the contingency/situational approaches, due to its ease of use across different levels of an organization and its prescriptive ability, is the Hersey-Blanchard Situational Leadership theory (1988). The model is based on a continuum of supportive or directive behavior, coupled with a continuum of the skills or maturity in the followers in the context of a given situation. According to Hersey-Blanchard, a leader's style and engagement with followers is contingent on the ability of the followers (1988). The main weakness of the model is the reliance of the leader to assess the ability of both the individual and groups to adjust styles quickly.

However, an advantage of the contingency/situational approach is the prescriptive abilities for leader engagement. For instance, you can expect that in the initial stages of an operation, if you are employing less skilled personnel, an authoritarian style may aid in task organization and completion. This was true in Natural Fire 10 due to the cross-sectional design of our team. The members' individual skills were high but as a group, they were not efficient at working together during initial formation. As work commenced and the Task Force Kitgum team became more mature in their activities, the leadership style changed to a delegative style in order to better support team member growth. You will see this perspective expanded upon to guide leadership strategies during various phases of a mission.

Power and Influence Approaches

A leadership phenomenon present across the trait, behavioral and contingency/situational approaches is the existence of power and ability to influence others. The *power* and *influence* theories are based on the manner in which leadership influence is applied. Researchers have identified several approaches and forms of influence that may be employed by leaders to obtain results.

Perhaps the simplest influence approach is transactional leadership. Transactional leadership presumes that all influence is based on task and reward structures. More specifically, influence is derived through a designated transaction between work and benefits. A clear example is the pay one receives for work with additional compensation for overtime effort. A normal pay for work transaction provides a baseline of effort associated with specified payments. However, exceeding the expected transaction (work for pay) at the same rate

Table 2.3

French & Raven's Five Forms of Power

Positional Power	Personal Power
Legitimate	Expert
Reward	Referent
Coercive	

often does not incentivize increased effort. Instead, greater compensation (or reward) is offered for output that exceeds the baseline (hours or holidays) providing the influence to increase effort.

Another approach, named after its researchers, is French & Raven's Five Forms of Power (1989). This model identified five types of power and placed them within two categories: *positional* and *personal*. Within the positional power category, a leader can employ *legitimate, reward,* and *coercive* types of power to influence people whom they have authority over. For the personal power category, the model identified *expert* and *referent* (the influence referred onto a leader by the team member) types of power as influencers.

According to research on French & Raven's Five Forms of Power, *personal* power has emerged as the most beneficial category of influence. Within the category of personal power, *expert* power is often designated as the best type of influence (Bass, 1990). Expert power is the concept of leading by example, or role modeling. Most people are quick to recognize the influence that comes from expertise and demonstrating the behaviors expected of others. Expert and referent influence are strongly associated with credibility and trust, two psychosocial bonds that enhance the willingness to follow leaders.

As the 560th BFSB team prepared for our role in Natural Fire 10, we knew that we would have to exercise influence through positional power but also rely on personal power in order to have an effective organization. Our identification as the lead element for

Task Force Kitgum provided the positional related influence over the units assigned to the force. We also had the benefit of higher-ranking personnel among our team providing each having some form of legitimate influence based on rank. However, with a joint and multinational force such as Task Force Kitgum, the positional power was diminished because of the temporary nature of the operation combined with limited real authority over participants. Subsequently, we knew we could rely on positional influence initially and to a point, but our goal became to influence through expert and referent power through the mission.

Transformational Leadership

In addition to the four main theoretical approaches to leadership, a term that has gained much ground over the last two decades is *transformational leadership*. Transformational is made from two words: (1) *'trans,'* or "to move," and (2) *'form,'* meaning a "structure or model." Transformation is therefore *moving from one shape to another*. Transformational leadership refers to the role a leader has in influencing the purpose and process of transformation. This term is an important concept in many corporations and is often associated with continuous improvement initiatives.

At its core, transformational leadership involves connecting a leader to its members in a manner that raises the consciousness of individuals and improves their commitment to the organization (Bass, 2005). Transformational leaders need to be visionary and be able to communicate a collective interest that unites organizational members. The leader's vision is often associated with individual improvement, empowerment and values, all of which create a sense of self-efficacy among members (Northouse, 1997).

Transformational leadership encompasses a broad range of leader behaviors and skills that describe how a leader can initiate action, develop members and carry out significant change in an organization. Essentially, a transformational leader will instill a sense of purpose, direction and belief that a new way is possible. The leader will seek to implement changes that will improve the organization and its members. Natural Fire 10 was an example of transformational leadership in action. We intended to accomplish our mission and ensure that all the participants, including our own team, were positively affected by the experience.

For military planning purposes, the description and definition of success for a mission is articulated in a statement referred to as the *commander's intent*. Its purpose is both to inform planning as well as help organizational members understand what is to be achieved as the mission unfolds. I tried to capture my intent and expected outcomes for Natural Fire 10 in a manner that fused the main tasks with the Task Force participants, the participants with one another, and the value to all including the Task Force members, their respective countries and the local community. For this important operation and all its complexities, I had to develop a simple but succinct way of communicating my transformational vision for Task Force Kitgum. The vision had to be easily understood by a wide audience of joint and coalition partner. Thus, my commander's intent stated:

> COMMANDER'S INTENT: Natural Fire 10 is intended to improve response and operational capabilities of partner nations and U.S. forces; Task Force Kitgum will be the tactical component. I intend to fully integrate multinational partners into the Task Force staff, synchronize and execute Field Training Exercise (FTX) and Humanitarian and Civic Assistance (HCA) operations in a realistic and safe environment, and support with a joint logistics center. We will build relationships with our multinational partners, share tactics techniques and procedures (TTP's), enhance the interoperability among participating forces and put an African face on all operations.

<u>ENDSTATE:</u> Task Force Kitgum, successfully conducted multinational training and HCA in the Kitgum AO. All participants have an increased understanding of each other's capabilities and strengths, and the importance of transparency, rule of law, and strengthening democratic institutions. All FTX participants completed 100% of individual tasks to standard. Specified medical and educational facilities have been improved. Regional medical personnel have increased ability and over 10,000 local citizens have been provided medical and dental care. Strategic and tactical communications nets were fully operational throughout the duration of the exercise. Task Force Kitgum elements received all necessary resources/support to complete mission requirements. All participants redeployed safely, and interoperability among partner nations has been enhanced.

The commander's intent statement tells a story. To take the story into action requires a leadership approach that brings people to an understanding of value and belief that the end-state is both possible and worth the effort. The commander's intent statement for Natural Fire 10 is a good example of a transformational leadership approach: we will be focused on Kitgum, do things together, support one another, learn from each other, accomplish our missions, and both the Task Force members and the people of Kitgum will be better off for it! The overarching approach is transformational in that we will all arrive in Kitgum in one "form" and evolve (or move) to a higher "form," and therefore depart improved.

One of the basic tenets of transformational leadership and reason for its popular appeal, is the emphasis on role modeling. Leaders are compelled to model the values and behaviors expected from others in the organization, thus providing a moral authority to influence members. Transformational leadership places a strong emphasis on the needs and growth of individuals. Particular investments are applied to the members through education, training, experiential (specialized) assignments, coaching and accountability (Bass, 2005). The underlying assumption for the individual focus is as your team gets better, your organizational performance increases.

A recurring challenge of applying the tenets of transformational leadership is that leaders sometimes fail to model the behavior they expect from their people. Leaders must ensure that as members grow and become more educated, ethical, and experienced, they themselves also continue to rise. Where leaders often stumble in this approach is when they fail to improve themselves while attempting to encourage and improve others. The result can lead to a situation where employees' abilities continue to grow and ultimately surpass the leaders, thus creating the potential for dissatisfaction and loss of influence.

To be a transformational leader you must live what you believe. It is not about catchy phrases and visionary presentations. You must role model the behaviors you want others to emulate in the organization, grow in kind and engage yourself in the activities you are putting your people through, and demonstrate that you can live up to the standards expected of them. It goes back to taking the first step and then more afterwards, and with each additional foot forward demonstrating the behavior you expect of others. Remember that people are following you. The influence you build by role modeling is significant and will be recognized and manifested far beyond what you would believe.

Thoughts for Applying Leadership Theories

One thing we can ascertain after reviewing the main theoretical approaches to leadership is that there is no single best solution to leading people. You cannot behave your way into successful leadership and you cannot skill your way there. Instead, you need to employ a multidimensional approach that fits the needs of the mission, your people and the organization. For example, you should recognize and understand what your followers expect of you as a leader from the *trait* approach. You need to appreciate your people and their perspectives, abilities, strengths and weaknesses, and vary your style of leadership based on your people and the situation as noted through the *behavioral* and *situational/contingency* approaches. You can predict that at least initially you may be able to rely on your position, rank or authority to yield some level of influence over others. However, your expertise and how you engage your team will ultimately deliver the influence they need and the results your organization requires as noted from the *power and influence* approach. Diverse organizations and complex situations will challenge your capacity to lead; therefore, you should continuously work to improve your leadership skills and model the behaviors sought of others from the *transformational* approach.

My personal leadership philosophy of "A leader's role is to make others successful," best fits with the transformational approach with its intention of improving the organization through its people and action. The visioning and role modeling aspects of transformational leadership are particularly useful for setting the direction of an organization and demonstrating how to operate and achieve success. There is wide recognition that the best influence is not just what you say, but what you do. There is truth to the old adage, "Our actions speak louder than any word."

While commanding the 560th BFSB, I served a wide audience of specialized intelligence, reconnaissance, and support personnel. One group in particular, the paratroopers from the Long Range Surveillance (LRS) and Quartermaster (Rigger) units constantly forced me to demonstrate my expertise and role model certain "Lead from the front" behaviors. This despite chronic injuries from a somewhat hard life (over 28 years of service, 18 years spent in Airborne, LRS and Special Forces organizations).

As a brigade commander, it may have been unnecessary from a technical standpoint to continue to conduct airborne operations, but every scheduled jump I performed jumpmaster duties and made parachute jumps with the teams. I was one of the more experienced and senior jumpers in the brigade and designated leader. I had an obligation to lead by action, endure hardships with the Soldiers, and place myself in environments where I could directly interact with them. In addition to my role as a commander, several members of the brigade staff were placed on jump status as well to put them into a position of influence and direct participation with the brigade's Soldiers. One of whom, a female Lieutenant Colonel, serving as the 560th BFSB S3 (and for Natural Fire 10 the Task Force Executive Officer) provided another influencer. As a middle-aged mother donning her parachute and exiting helicopters and airplanes, she inspired the female paratroopers and pushed the male jumpers by her example.

Physically, the outcomes of my airborne jumps were always bad. They provided my wife with an excellent opportunity to chastise me when I stumbled into the house and fell straight onto our couch. Mentally, my perspective never changed despite the injuries – if you are going to be the leader, then lead by example or get out of the way. I recognized early on in my career there would be times when I could not be with Soldiers doing their jobs, so when I could participate with them I did so in ways that were meant to build trust and confidence.

Just prior to participating in Natural Fire, I made the last HALO parachute jumps of my career at Fort Carson, CO. My alma mater, the 10th Special Forces Group (Airborne), had graciously assigned an experienced HALO Jumpmaster to run me through the paces for free-fall parachuting currency. For two days I practiced to the point of proficiency in safety procedures for mishaps and malfunctions. Satisfied with my progress, the Jumpmaster and I drove out to a nearby drop zone in order to "strap hang" (a term for adding people onto an existing parachute operation) with a Special Forces HALO team. The day was beautiful and clear, perfect for making jumps from 18,000 feet (with oxygen) from the ramp of a C23 Sher-

pa aircraft.

This experience was much different than my first HALO impression. With well over 300 military jumps in all types of conditions it did not seem unnatural to leap off the ramp of the small transport aircraft at a high altitude. Although it continued to be a thrill to feel the winds and more im-

Figure 2.2. HALO jumpmaster spots drop zone from 18,000 feet on my final freefall in the U.S. Army. Photo by Author.

portantly, establish a stable position in free-fall. We made multiple jumps and following our successful landings would collect our gear and repack parachutes for the next opportunity to go again.

Between jumps I was rigging my parachute next to a young Staff Sergeant from the HALO team who was doing the same. We naturally struck up a conversation as I had once been a staff sergeant

on a Special Forces HALO team (ODA 044) prior to being commissioned as an officer. I asked him how long he had been on the HALO team and he responded only a few months. He continued by proudly exclaiming he had recently completed HALO school and this was the first time jumping with his new team. He looked

Figure 2.3. Feeling like an "old man" packing my HALO parachute. Photo by Author.

over at me and asked when I had completed HALO school. I paused before answering. I could tell it was probable the young noncommissioned officer may not have been born yet when I graduated the Military Free-fall Parachutist Course. I blurted out "1985" almost knowing the response. He stated with a smirk, "Yep, I wasn't even born yet." It served to reinforce my lovely wife's rebukes regarding my continued jumping. Thankfully the comment also was a reminder that leading isn't just about physically stepping forward but also mentally leaping ahead. At least I wasn't too old for that!

CHAPTER THREE

Concepts Every Leader Should Understand

As the 560th BFSB prepared for the operation in Uganda, we understood from the beginning that several overarching themes would play important roles in the success of Natural Fire 10. This operation was part of a theater engagement strategy by AFRICOM to improve relations and working protocols in East Africa. Engagement is the process of building commitment through communications and relationships. The Natural Fire 10 mission meant assembling an ad hoc group of people representing diverse organizations into a structure without formal command and control procedures. In situations such as this, you have to rely on "goodwill" to make things work. Thus, we were determined to place relationship building and communications processes at the forefront of our planning activities. These efforts were designed to bridge potential differences, open dialogue at every opportunity, and among all echelons of the military hierarchy.

Optimally, during this preparatory phase of the mission, I would have preferred a formal engagement strategy that involved direct meetings with all of the key leaders involved in Natural Fire 10. My experiences in multinational, multiagency, multicultural and multi-jurisdictional operations have yielded this truth regarding dialogue among participants - there is no better way to communicate than face-to-face when working with other people on complex requirements. Unfortunately, the compressed time and distance precluded the preferred course of action and instead we began the process by opening various channels and opportunities to collaborate electronically by telephone, email and an online communications portal called Defense Connect Online (DCO). DCO would serve us well with its voice, chat, and presentation options. Initially, our focus was with the higher commands of USARAF located in Vicenza, Italy and AFRICOM stationed in Stuttgart, Germany. The majority of higher-level decisions, coordination and resource allocations would be made between these two headquarters to support Natural Fire 10 including the movement of personnel and material into the area of operations.

In addition to the time differences and distances working with USARAF and AFRICOM, we also had engagement with active, reserve and National Guard units located across the U.S. and overseas. If the compressed schedule wasn't limiting enough for us to exercise a dynamic relationship and communications strategy with our partner organizations, we also found ourselves in the last quarter of the federal fiscal year (the U.S. Government uses 1 October – 30 September as the fiscal year for funding and resource allocations). This meant that funding wasn't available for a large-scale circulation plan to meet with leaders from the units we would ultimately be working with in Uganda. We prioritized accordingly and were determined to make two key meetings within that last 30 days leading up to the operation deemed significant to the mission. The first was with the commander and key personnel at USARAF in Vicenza, Italy and the other was with the largest element of our proposed Task Force, the U.S. Marine military police force in Minneapolis, MN.

The two trips were not only important for developing personal relationships among key personnel but they also communicated and demonstrated the leadership philosophy being employed – our job is to make others successful. Despite the authoritative position of the 560th BFSB regarding the Task Force's potential operations in Uganda, we chose to take ourselves to their locations as deference to their respective roles and demonstrate that our role was to be of service to them. It was our intent to demonstrate by action that our job was to make them successful and not their job to make us a success in the mission.

The trips were the start of a continuous effort to model the leadership behaviors and the philosophy we wanted to see employed throughout the mission. The Marine commander initially wondered why would the 560th BFSB leadership team visit and what value would it be this late in the preparation for the mission? Afterwards, she acknowledged that it was invaluable to alleviating her and her command's apprehensions regarding roles, the command relationship, and intent for the mission. This was one step to begin the process of building an organizational culture for Task Force Kitgum.

The leadership traits, styles, and skills employed through an operation can help achieve results but the relationships established through interpersonal communication, collaboration and problem-solving will be the sustaining elements of the team. An important theory for guiding the development of relationships and effective communications is the *expectancy theory*. The theory is built upon the premise that every act will be followed by an outcome. A person's motivation to act is based on the value they place on the expected outcome (Vroom, 1964). There are three components to expectancy theory:

☐ Expectancy or degree of confidence a person has with regard to their ability to accomplish a desired behavior.
☐ Instrumentality or degree of confidence a person has that if the desired behavior is demonstrated they will be rewarded appropriately.
☐ Valence or the value a person places in the expected rewards.

The model assumes that people will be motivated and exhibit behaviors based on the expectancies of the outcome of their actions. Their strength of motivation and influence on behavior is linked to the value assigned or perceived by the outcome. The value, or *valence*, is directly related to the preference or needs of the individual (Yeatts & Hyten, 1998). Here is an example of expectancy theory in action:

> Suppose for a moment that you value or really enjoy entertainment, particularly action movies. While watching TV you view an exciting commercial depicting highlights of an upcoming movie release. You are motivated to action based on the preview you saw and prepare to attend a movie premiere at a local theater. You plan with your significant other to attend, set aside the resources, schedule a baby sitter, go out to dinner, purchase tickets, purchase refreshments and find yourself in the theater, all based on the expectation that you will be entertained.

The movie example is pretty straightforward and the objective of most marketing campaigns. Now let us transition to the "other" part of expectancy theory. Specifically, why it is so valuable for leader understanding and what is the impact on perceived satisfaction and dissatisfaction? Using the movie story, what do you think the response would be if the movie was superb or if it ended as a flop? Suppose the movie was excellent and lived up to its previews, one would assume the viewer would be satisfied. However you cannot guarantee satisfaction by meeting expectations because the instrumentality that brought you there may impact your perception. For instance, if you paid for the baby sitter, took your significant other out to dinner, bought tickets and refreshments, and found yourself having spent $150 to watch a movie, the reward of entertainment may not have been worth the instrumentality required to obtain the outcome. On the other hand, if the movie was horrible you can definitely guarantee dissatisfaction. Therein lies the value of understanding expectancy theory: if you meet or exceed peoples' expectations you cannot guarantee satisfaction, however if you do not meet their expectations you can always guarantee dissatisfaction.

Expectancy theory is a powerful motivation theory and communication is the key to avoiding the potential for dissatisfaction. Every leadership approach, style and behavior is part of a communicative process that takes ideas, translates them to expectancies, and ultimately provides valence for member motivation. It is important to recognize that while you as the leader have expectations of employee work, they also have expectations of your performance. If you recall from the trait approach, the characteristics of *intelligence, self-confidence, determination, integrity,* and *sociability* are thought to be the traits most influential to followers. To some extent, these traits can be considered follower expectancies of a leader's behavior. As a leader your ability to meet these basic characteristics may not guarantee the satisfaction of your team members but not living up to these expectations will likely lead to dissatisfaction of you as a leader.

Whether you are a leader or team member the simplest method of identify the expectations of others is to open a dialogue. Communication helps provide a common or shared understanding of what is being attempted and enables people to meet or exceed expectations. A basic human assumption associated with performance is most people want to succeed at what they are doing. However, in many cases the criteria for success is unclear and differs from one person to another. If you find yourself dissatisfied with the performance of another or when you or your people fail to meet the expectations of others consider asking yourself these three questions:

- ☐ Did they understand the behaviors expected?
- ☐ Could they perform the required behavior?
- ☐ Did they just not do it?

If you cannot answer the first two questions as a leader you have likely caused the insufficient behavior as a result of your inability to communicate the expectancies, instrumentality and valence of the requirement to the person performing the work. Any dissatisfaction you feel regarding their effort should be considered dissatisfaction in your own leadership abilities. It is important to note the ability to communicate and then meet or exceed subsequent expectations is the foundation from which trust and relationships are built. Open communication is key for common understanding and realizing the potential for people to exceed expectations.

While expectancy theory and its relation to satisfaction and dissatisfaction can inform leader behavior, one must recognize that those feelings are temporal attitudes. Indeed some researchers have argued that focusing on satisfaction is irrelevant as long as people are doing their job (Meyer & Allen, 1993). Instead, leaders should be more concerned with developing *commitment*, a concept decidedly different than developing satisfaction. Meyer and Allen (1991) identified commitment as "a psychological state that characterizes the relationship between the employee and organization and has implications for continued membership" (p.67).

Commitment is a global concept and reflects a general response to an organization whereby satisfaction is more of a task-related concept reflecting one's response to certain aspects of work (Meyer & Allen, 1991). Commitment is therefore more stable over time unlike the transitory events that result in one being either satisfied or dissatisfied during daily events.

There are three constructs associated with organizational commitment and they are *affective, continuance* and *normative commitment*. Affective commitment is an employee's positive emotional attachment to an organization. Affective commitment refers to how much you 'like' the organization. Continuance commitment is derived from the cost of disassociation from an organization. Essentially continuance speaks to your perceived loss from disassociation. Normative commitment refers to one's feeling of obligation to remain in an organization. This is akin to living up to your obligations to stay aligned with your organization (Meyer & Allen, 1997). The three commitment constructs are not mutually exclusive and employees are likely to have a multidimensional affiliation with their organizations that may change over time.

48

There are three aspects of commitment that are important drivers of a leader's behavior. The first is to recognize employees generally desire to be psychologically committed to something. Their alternative to commitment is alienation, which is thought to be unhealthy (Kobasa, Maddi, & Kahn, 1982). The second part of putting commitment research to action is to understand that among the three constructs of commitment, the strongest for affiliation purposes is believed to be affective commitment. Finally, the third aspect concerns the impacts of locally committed employees, over those who identify globally committed (both local and global), or are uncommitted. Specifically, when employees are locally committed to their supervisor and work group the outcomes include higher job satisfaction, performance and pro-social behaviors (Becker & Billings, 1993). As a leader, you want to build affective commitment with your team members and not rely on the weaker constructs of continuance or normative commitment to sustain membership.

An important leadership role in any context is relationship building. Returning to the tenets of the expectancy theory, your development of value, or valence, in the mission is important for both motivating team members to action and also developing a shared sense of purpose for the mission. In joint military terms, a shared sense of purpose is referred to as *unity of effort* (Joint Publication 3.0, 2011). This shared purpose will help members overcome cultural or other boundaries and assist in relationship building. Strong relationships built on met expectancies are an antecedent to affective commitment in your organization or to your mission. This equation will sustain your team during those daily events as they yield periods of satisfaction or dissatisfaction with the environment or aspects of the work.

SECTION TWO

Leading an Organization

CHAPTER FOUR

Organizational Culture and the Role of Leaders

The leadership role for Natural Fire 10's tactical element, Task Force Kitgum, would not be an easy task. Our team from the 560th BFSB would need to embrace and assimilate the differences among the U.S. components (Army, Navy, Air Force and Marines) including the different rank insignia, lingo, business rules and behavioral norms. More challenging would be to understand and incorporate the military traditions of the partner nations of Burundi, Kenya, Rwanda, Tanzania and Uganda. In addition to bringing together the military cultures of the U.S joint forces and the five additional East African countries, we also had to contend with language barriers, customs, business approaches, and values. Therefore as the 560th BFSB prepared the operational plans for Natural Fire 10, we simultaneously readied for the working environment that we would be required to form upon arrival in Uganda. Our Natural Fire 10 setting would involve creating an overarching organizational culture that could work in concert with and not against the cultural elements we would be assimilating. Fortunately, the 560th BFSB had been in the culture building cycle of organizational development for the preceding two years.

In 2007, the 560th BFSB was "stood up" as the first BFSB in the Army. The unit was among many new or redesigned Army brigades meant for decentralized and non-contiguous operations against future enemies. The Army's idea was to build a capability-based force that was task organized to fit unique and non-linear battlefields. The prevailing wisdom was that our potential enemies would not likely

53

face off against the U.S. in large-scale battles across open terrain. Instead, they would disperse and operate in environments that would provide them a tactical advantage including operating in heavily populated urban areas. Infantry and other combat arms brigades would be necessary to provide security and hold ground while intelligence and reconnaissance capabilities were deemed necessary to cover the gaps. Protecting the areas between brigades or reinforcing those brigades' ability to understand and pinpoint adversaries would be the role of the new BFSB.

The new BFSB consisted of a headquarters company for command and control of the brigades' personnel and assets. There were two brigade-enterprise support units: a brigade support company for maintenance and logistics, and a signal company to provide the communications infrastructure for the organization. The BFSB had two maneuver battalions to support its intelligence collection mission. The first consisting of a military intelligence battalion packed with signals intelligence (SIGINT), human intelligence (HUMINT), and counterintelligence (CI) experts. The second battalion was a cavalry squadron with mounted (on vehicles) and dismounted (on foot) reconnaissance soldiers including an airborne LRS company.

The 560th BFSB had very little official doctrine to direct its initial formation. As a leader, it is infrequent to have an opportunity to start a business or stand-up a new organization from scratch, particularly one in the Army. More often you enter an existing organization with the intent and desire to make a difference. This requires a period of assessment where you observe and ask questions to determine how you can make an impact, how you can help people realize their potential, and how you can improve the results of your company. This is a normal inquisitive process to determine what is happening, why things are occurring and how choices and behaviors are being influenced. In many cases you find yourself attempting to interpret culture without recognizing the existence of an organizational culture.

Edgar Schein authored a superb book to help leaders decipher and navigate corporate behavior entitled "Organizational Culture and Leadership" now in its third edition (2004). Schein defined *organizational culture* as " a pattern of shared assumptions that the group learned as it solved problems of external adaptation and internal integration, that has worked well enough to be considered valid and, therefore, to be taught to new members as the correct way to perceive, think, and feel in relation to problems" (p.17). His definition was derived from common themes found in anthropological research such as observing roles, norms, performance, shared meanings, habits of thinking, rewards, punishment, patterning and integration among group members.

The value of assessing organizational culture is it helps decipher why people behave in various organizational situations. Seeing people exhibit a willingness to sacrifice for others, observing certain groups routinely achieve high performance, experiencing situations where seemingly rational team members do something absolutely out of context begs the questions: "Why are they doing that or why would they do that?" I'm sure you've heard verbal clues without recognition that they represented cultural patterning. "That's the way we do it around here." "We've always done it that way." "We had a person who did things like this all the time and always got away with it." "I would not worry about that, we don't care about doing that procedure or adhering to that policy." Those expressions are indicators that cultural elements are at work and impacting the norms and behaviors of the group.

Deciphering verbal and non-verbal cues involves identifying and understanding the interaction between the three layers of organizational culture: *artifacts, espoused values* and *underlying assumptions*. Each of the layers provides clues about the influences at work driving organizational behavior. We would connect these layers in a congruent manner to build the culture of the 560th BFSB.

The top band of culture and most readily apparent are organizational artifacts. Artifacts are those things that are observed, intuitively felt, and help frame the organization by the viewer. When a person enters a new organizational setting they make immediate judgments based on their observations. For example, if you were to walk into a restaurant and note unclean tables, overflowing garbage cans, and witness poor customer service you are likely to draw some conclusions about your potential experience or the food quality. If you visited a law enforcement or military organization and witnessed the facilities, vehicles, weapons and uniforms in disrepair, you may make a judgment about their discipline or effectiveness. In both cases you are conducting surface observations of organizational artifacts and beginning the process of forming a value judgment. A leader's goals regarding artifacts are to make an initial impression and convey the right message to a viewer.

One artifact unique to military organizations and purposed to identify assigned members is the distinctive unit insignia (unit patch). It is rare to get the opportunity to design an Army patch but our new BFSB presented one of those infrequent occurrences. We quickly began developing a patch and motto to serve as a continuous reminder of what the 560th BFSB symbolized. Artwork was requested from newly assigned people in the brigade and a collaborative process was used to vote on the best designs. The final version was shaped as a Greek spear tip to signify the weapons of the earliest elite warriors and the importance of the brigade's intelligence as the "tip of the spear" for directing the force behind it. Inside the spear tip was a dagger symbolizing the sharpness and technical and tactical proficiency of the brigade's soldiers. Half the patch was light blue representing the brigade's long range reconnaissance capabilities, while the other half was black denoting the unknown characteristics of the future battlefields. A lightning bolt is depicted striking into the black illustrating the brigade's mission of delivering intelligence and analogous of providing light in darkness. We designated our brigade motto, "To the Point," to verbally denote the role we served as the tip of the intelligence spear. It also represented the manner we would report information internally and externally to the brigade – no wasted time and always direct.

Except for the patch worn daily by unit members on their uniforms, most of the 560th BFSB's artifacts were found in our first headquarters building. We were initially housed (now relocated to a modern facility) inside a World War II era brick warehouse. It was a fairly nondescript building from an outside perspective but we wanted visitors to quickly see they were in a high performance organization upon entry. The main foyer was adorned with the unit insignia and "To the Point" motto. Also displayed were unit flags, photos of unique worldwide operations, gifts from other countries military organizations whom we had worked, upcoming events, high scores from fitness tests, and other examples of excellence. Each artifact was purposefully added to ensure both visitors and organizational members were exposed to the wide range of missions, upcoming events, and excellence of the personnel assigned.

Another preliminary perception rendered by people as they enter an organization is how space is allocated. Looking at floor plans and furniture may sound trivial, but it offers much about stature, importance, and communications. The location and proximity to supervisors, special accommodations for senior managers, openness of floor plans, and cubicle arrangements all send subtle messages to the viewer. Even the type and placement of furniture sends a message regarding the relationships between people. For instance, if you were to walk into an office and find yourself immediately blocked by a desk and chair, there is indication the person wants separation from those who may come in for assistance. Closed doors often imply "do not come in" and may suggest either a need for quiet or a desire for isolation from the workforce. We positioned the commander's office directly accessible from the 560th BFSB entry foyer and routinely kept the door open, and desk positioned in a way to encourage people to come in. The entire entry area was designed to draw visitors into the organization and open the opportunity for communication. While initial perceptions such as the examples here provide context, you should not draw conclusions from simple viewpoints. The next layer of organizational culture goes a step beyond what is observed and sensed.

The next level of analysis provides a deeper understanding of the group's focus and activities by delving into the *espoused values* of the organization. Espoused values are items that literally and figuratively communicate an organization's purpose, values, and items of importance. Assessing espoused values involve reviewing policies, mission and vision statements, values, strategies, standards, and procedures employed by the organization. For example the 560th BFSB's motto, "To the Point," was an espoused value as well as related to our unit's mission (being the intelligence tip of the spear), an aspect of our values (candor), and leading from the front.

In addition to the motto we valued teamwork across our formation in part because intelligence collection does not rely on a single source of information. Instead cuing and redundancy are sought to validate and back up assessments. While the 560th BFSB articulated teamwork as a value, teamwork is always a challenging for organizations to operationalize. Teamwork is easier communicated than codified since companies rarely deviate from individualized evaluations, pay, assignments, and other human resource systems that support individualized recognition and reward. When faced with a value undermined or unsupported by corporate systems and processes, you have to design your own mechanism to support or reinforce the value. For the 560th BFSB, teamwork was routinely expressed by our arrangement of units and training exercises designed to encourage working together and being responsible to support one another. When you assess an espoused value always look at how your structures or systems of the organization either help or hurt your desired behavior.

One important and often overlooked part of deciphering

organizational culture is through a review of budget and resource allocations. Where and how money is spent provides volumes of information about perceived value in parts of the organization. For instance, if your company espouses "People are our greatest resource," but instead of applying fiscal resources to improve employee training, pay, and benefits, money is spent on buying items of limited organizational value. There may be some incongruence between word and deed. As a new BFSB, our organization focused resources at building individual and collective capabilities keeping with the individualized focus of transformational leadership. That is, through the people the organization improves and thrives. Always look at the organizational budget as a significant statement of priorities that can be utilized to assess the values of a corporation.

As the 560th BFSB evolved, we were very cognizant of our resources and building capabilities. However, we firmly believed that our organization capabilities would increase only as a result of increasing technical qualifications and experiences of the exceptional people assigned and recruited to fill the unit. This perspective allowed us to devote the majority of our resources to sending people to schools, training and on operations. Our assumption was we could always obtain materials or equipment in a timely manner but getting people with specialized training or a language in time to support a contingency mission was almost impossible. Therefore, our effort went into training and certifying people who could add value when placed into any situation. The lesson for leaders is to make every effort to associate espoused values with systems and resources to ensure words and actions are aligned.

The third layer of organizational culture and perhaps the hardest to influence are the *underlying assumptions* of the members. Underlying assumptions are essentially "truths" learned and reinforced over a period of time. At the individual level, a person's behavior is guided by a complex system of cognitive learning. A person's background and experiences from family interactions, community involve-

...ıent, formal and informal education, religious/spiritual upbringing, and peer influences all produce a value scheme that directs an individual action. An individual's unconscious perceptions, thoughts and feelings are antecedents that guide moral decision-making. Underlying assumptions are critical for assessing an organization's culture because they are thought to be the basis for decision making by both the individuals and the corporate body. When you observe seemingly rational people acting irrationally and out of character from what the organization espouses, looking deeper into their underlying assumptions is often telling.

It is important to remember that organizations are made up of human beings and therefore leading an organization involves leading people. People bring all their personal assumptions into the organizational context and can influence corporate behavior. Leaders must be cognizant of their role in promoting and fostering an environment that shapes organizational truths. Early in an organization's development the leaders will serve as the primary drivers of culture formation. Most problems will have direct participation by the leaders whose problem solving will be patterned as issues related to internal integration and external adaption follow. As new members are integrated into the organization these basic assumptions guide the development of norms and performance. Managers and leaders who embody the corporate values and thinking will perpetuate the patterns of the organizations and will be advanced accordingly. In essence, leaders create culture early in the lifecycle of an organization and later in the culture of organization to create its future leaders.

A leader's values and actions are imbued into an organization's culture through *primary* and *secondary imbedding mechanisms*. An imbedding mechanism refers to a process or method for implanting ideals into the thoughts of organizational members. *Primary imbedding mechanisms* are action-based and send a significant message of "truth" to the members of what is valued. One of the most powerful techniques for leaders to communicate preferences and values are through what they care about and pay attention to. Another important imbedding mechanism is the criteria that leaders use to select, promote, assign, excommunicate and retire members.

Early in the formation of the 560th BFSB one of the first requirements was to fill the vacant positions with personnel. Understanding the value of effective leadership, role modeling and the influence of primary imbedding mechanisms to organizational culture, I initially hand selected each member for key positions in the brigade. So despite the organization operating without approved doctrine and awaiting the bulk of its new equipment, we did possess a small group of proven leaders who relished the challenge of developing a new organization with high standards and a strong professional ethic. What they produced during this timeframe was a high performance culture with an expectation of success.

By the time the unit became involved with Natural Fire 10, much of what was written on employing a BFSB headquarters was born out of unique missions the 560th BFSB participated. The organization grew from the original two people on the unit's manning document, to over 1,000 Soldiers with a wide variety of specialties. Despite the fact the unit was "standing up" in Army lexicon, the leadership of the organization took every opportunity to challenge its people and processes. This included deploying people and command elements to over 15 countries during the first two years of the 560th BFSB's existence and developing lessons and new employment doctrine at every opportunity.

Each new mission that surfaced for the 560th BFSB offered an opportunity to establish criteria that reinforced the standards sought from our membership. For instance, when selecting members for the Natural Fire 10 team, every person had to be qualified, medically screened, have passed fitness and weapons qualification, along with several other basic Soldier standards expected of everyone in the brigade. Had we chose people who did not meet the basic standards, a mixed message would have been sent to membership. Leader choices associated with human resource decisions are especially significant for communicating clear messages on desired behavior.

Secondary imbedding mechanisms should reinforce the primary mechanisms. These include espoused values such as the mission, vision, values, and policies of the organization. A technique for leaders to reinforce functional and supportive corporate climate, is to nest their vision, objectives and expectancies into each echelon of the organization. Understanding these elements helps organizational members know how their individual and collective effort supports the corporate mission and vision. Leaders who espouse values and institutionalize systems to support and reinforce higher-level purpose will create congruency between what they "say" and how the organization functions. For example, one of the 560th BFSBs corporate values was teamwork. By selecting members from across the brigade to serve as the Task Force headquarters in Natural Fire 10, we executed a team approach to the mission connecting value of teamwork to an action by selecting a cross-section of brigade members.

The influence organizational culture has on individual and corporate decision-making and behavior can be significant. Explaining why organizations and their people behave is one of the main reasons for looking at this phenomenon. Leaders at all levels must be cognitive of their role and the way they change or reinforce organizational culture. Your challenge is to strive for a set of conditions whereby everything that members observe, express, experience, and believe are patterned together in a manner that supports organizational goals.

Word + Action = Truth

Creating *congruence* is the key for connecting the organization together in a positive manner. Congruency refers to the functional alignment of artifacts, espoused values and underlying assumptions. Dysfunction occurs when *incongruence* exists between layers of culture. For leadership, there is nothing more problematic than a new member learning about the mission, vision, values and policies of an organization from their supervisor, only to have a co-worker make a statement like: "Everything the boss said is irrelevant, what we really believe around here is this." Or, "That may be the written standard, but this is how we get around it to get the job done." Statements such as these are a clear indication that incongruence exists and much akin to the alignment of an automobile, will likely drive individuals and your organization off course.

Therefore, it is important for leaders to ensure congruence exists between the three levels of organizational culture for consistency in message, action and thought. The convergence of word and action helps form the underlying assumptions and cognitive learning of the membership. Congruence among levels of culture thereby shape how members perceive and think. When the learned assumptions become "truths" and are taught to new members, the leader has begun to influence the culture of the organization.

Leaders also need to be cognizant of the important role they play in imbedding ethics and values into their organizational culture. Recognition of the three layers of culture and how they interact to influence behavior is important. However, a leader's action and involvement send the strongest message to organizational members and are critical for establishing an ethical and moral climate. Inconsistency between message and deed is extremely detrimental to a leader's credibility and undermines their ability to positively affect culture. Altering what people see and hear are the easy parts, changing the understanding and beliefs are more difficult and often take generations to break institutionalized schemas, or pre-formatted ways of solving problems (also known as bad habits). Leaders must recognize the influence derived from their actions and the strategic implications member responses can have on organizational culture.

The influence organizational culture has on individual and corporate decision-making and behavior can be significant. Explaining why organizations and their people behave is one of the main reasons for looking at this phenomenon. Leaders have an important role in developing, changing, or reinforcing organizational culture. Your challenge is to strive for a set of conditions whereby everything that members observe, express, experience, and believe are patterned together in a manner that supports organizational goals. Understanding the layers of organizational culture (artifacts, espoused values, underlying assumptions), the goal of congruency, the formula (Word + Action = Truth), and imbedding mechanisms will help strategically influence your organization's culture.

During the period leading up to Natural Fire 10, we were in the process of creating the culture of the 560th BFSB. The deliberate steps and strategies we employed to shape the behavior of the new brigade would serve us well for replicating similar actions to the Task Force we were developing and would employ during Natural Fire 10. In the following chapters you will see more examples of how we fused together various artifacts and espoused values to support patterns of behavior expected from all participants.

CHAPTER FIVE

Preparing to Lead an Operation

The U.S. military has devoted considerable time developing doctrine to guide leaders through a process of planning and executing of complex operations. Generally speaking, the preferred method of developing a detailed plan is to break it into segments or phases. A phase is a distinct point in a process designed to form something purposed to synchronize with something else. From a planning context, the phases are the segments that focus time and resources to develop your organization and the environment that allows you to be prepared and successful in succeeding phases. The military uses an Operations Order (OPORD) to capture and document the plan including all the phases and purposes to support the mission. A specific part of the OPORD entitled "concept of the operations" is to provide an overview of what is to occur throughout the mission, by whom, when and to what standard. One thing the U.S. military does not formally teach in the planning process is how to develop a leadership strategy to flow with the phasing of an operation and its requirements. This will be covered later in this section.

During the planning for Natural Fire 10, the command and staff developed a concept of operation to describe, in general terms, how the 560th BFSB would accomplish its mission from beginning to end. Natural Fire 10 was a complex operation and involved significant coordination with very little time or margin of error. For example, just getting our team into the country of Uganda required immunizations, official passports, country clearance, visas, a transportation plan including plane tickets, packing lists, security, medical screening and a host of other items. A purposeful effort ensued to identify requirements, essential tasks, key actions and break them into manageable work segments.

During the initial stages of any operation, one of a leader's roles is to create structure, organize work and allocate time to help communicate focus and build predictability. *Chunking* work together with clear starting and ending periods as well as specific standards provide employees a guide and leaders checkpoints along the way. One should also align work segments in a manner where they are tied together or build upon each other. When alignment is good and communicated to team members they can often see how what they are doing now has value in another or later segment in the process. For example, for entry into Uganda we were required to have an official passport, visa and country clearance. The completion of administrative tasks such as taking a passport photo, filling out a visa application, and other like requirements set the conditions for the person to successfully negotiate Ugandan customs and immigration service when they arrived for the mission. With the myriad of tasks necessary for the success of Natural Fire 10, our effort to segment was focused on simplifying the complicated. Thus we identified four phases that seemed to logically organize the work necessary to successfully execute our roles in Natural Fire 10: Pre-deployment, Deployment, On-site Operations, and Redeployment.

Phase I or pre-deployment, began immediately after being approved for the mission and ended on October 6, 2009. This date was when the Advanced Party for Natural Fire 10 was scheduled to depart the Atlanta airport on commercial aircraft through Europe and onto Entebbe Airport, Uganda. We identified that proper documents, travel arrangements, medical preparation, training and issuing specialized equipment were all critical elements for the success of Phase I. Subsequently all Soldiers participating in Natural Fire 10 would conduct an extensive administrative processing that included receiving official passports, country clearance, visas, in addition to updating next of kin and emergency information. The travel preparation included the scheduling of airline reservations for the advance party, while the main body required both commercial airline ticketing as well as contract air carrier coordination for personnel and equipment.

The phase one medical preparation was extensive and involved multiple presentations on the plethora of things that can kill you in Uganda as well as a significant round of immunizations. Our training plan included country and threat briefings, combatives (hand to hand combat practice), and familiarization with all the communications gear we were bringing to the operation. We were issued new and specialized equipment for the mission and we accounted for the materials, practiced with the items and packed them for the mission. Phase one was an important segment to set the conditions for later success and every detail was constantly checked, re-checked, rehearsed and every detail inspected.

Phase II or deployment, began on October 6, 2009 with the advance party departure from the Atlanta airport and ended on October 11, 2009 when the main body of the headquarters team arrived at Kitgum. The plan was for the advance party to depart Atlanta by commercial air on October 6th and arrive in Entebbe the next day October 7th. They would stay in Entebbe for two days then depart on October 9th by bus and arrive at Kitgum the same day. Meanwhile the main body would depart from the Atlanta airport and arrive at the Baltimore airport on October 8th. This group would then switch to a military charter aircraft and fly to Entebbe arriving on October 10th. Once in Uganda, the main body would spend the night on the Entebbe airfield then depart via CH47 Chinook helicopters and arrive in Kitgum on October 11th. The accountability and transfer of all personnel and equipment from the U.S. to Kitgum was deemed vital for the success of phase two.

Phase III, on-site operations, began on October 10th with the arrival of the main body in Uganda and ended when operations were complete in Kitgum. During this phase, participants were to establish a multi-national field TOC for Task Force Kitgum and conduct operations with partner nations. Task Force Kitgum would command and control the humanitarian and civic assistance as well as all security operations and training. The opening and closing ceremonies were included in this phase. Establishing and maintaining communications, and ensuring safe execution of operations were critical to the success of this phase.

Lastly, Phase IV or redeployment, would begin when operations were complete on October 27th and ended when all 560th BFSB Soldiers arrived safely at home station around October 30th. Upon mission completion, the team would travel as a group from Kitgum by CH47 helicopters to Entebbe airport, and then depart Entebbe by commercial air charter. Much like the deployment phase, accountability of personnel and equipment were deemed critical to the success of this phase.

Like the work of the staff of the 560th BFSB developing a plan for Natural Fire 10, each activity undertaken can be subdivided into phases to help organize work and time. If you are planning a mission trip to a foreign country or a team-building event in the mountains, you follow a similar set of steps (whether you realize it or not). Generally, you will start by developing a plan, preparing your people and equipment, and training for whatever tasks you are going to conduct. Knowing how to plan, prepare and train were the main requirements identified in our pre-deployment phase of Natural Fire 10. Next, you will travel to the location of the event, and stage your people and equipment to a site where they can work. This was the deployment phase of our mission to Uganda. Conducting your activity is synonymous to the on-site phase of Natural Fire 10. Recovering your people and equipment, returning from where you came, "refitting" or repairing materials, sharing lessons, and paying the bills can all be considered the redeployment phase for the purposes of Natural Fire 10.

Think about the phasing and requirements of a family camping trip. You will plan and schedule (plan), gather rations and equipment (prepare), perhaps practice a tent setup or test your propane stove (train), drive to the location (travel), remove your gear and unpack (stage), enjoy yourselves (conduct the mission), pack up (recover), drive home (return) and unpack and pay the bills (refit). For Natural Fire 10 we lumped many of these segments into four general phases but each could be its own stage for planning purposes. It is important to point out that whatever segmenting and phasing methodology you employ, phases are not normally mutually exclusive. Instead, they will often overlap and may be working simultaneously especially when executing a long-term complex mission. For instance, expanding on the camping scenario above, perhaps the scope moves from your immediate family and now includes leading a group trip. The complexity increased exponentially with multiple families preparing, traveling and arriving at different periods to the selected camping location. Despite the simultaneous actions of many families, phasing is still useful to characterize and guide the efforts of the group.

In addition to the value of segmenting portions of an operation for organizing and communicating, the process also has usefulness for leader preparation. As noted earlier in the text, your interpersonal skills can greatly assist you by adjusting your leadership styles to fit the situational or environmental factors and the competency levels of the people you are working with. In addition to the adjustments for the people, there are some structural aspects of each phase you should recognize to help you plan your leadership strategy. With each step in the process there is a general leadership style orientation you should consider as you prepare for your mission.

In the *planning* phase, leader involvement is required. Followers need clear guidance early on in a mission and a leader's role is to develop a vision, mission, objectives, and communicate their intent in a manner that engenders support for the operation. Leaders help structure the work and standards expected by the members and must be available to the team for constant tuning or reinforcement. During planning, particularly in a constrained time environment, requirements come quickly and members need access to the leader routinely for decisions and course adjustment. Your interaction and availability provide a support structure for work and help to build confidence for your members in both their efforts and in your ability.

As you begin *preparing* your people and equipment for a mission, the group needs you to demonstrate your adherence to standards that will enable the mission to succeed. Leaders who are visible preparing their personal administrative and equipment demonstrate by action the importance of these elements. This visibility can take the form of role modeling behaviors such as being the first to receive immunizations, first to have their packing list checked off and first to complete passport or visa application requirements. Being first also places the leader in a very influential position when it comes to preparation by putting them on the moral high ground to check other's work by having their actions already complete.

During the *training* phase of the mission, you address specific weaknesses and gaps or enhance proficiencies that your team members require to succeed in their tasks. Whether the activities should take the form of educational briefings or hands-on skills, the leader's active participation sends a clear message on the importance of the action. Additionally, this communicates the activity is a critical area where no deviation from standards are allowed. If you are practicing first aid, everyone including the leader needs to meet the standard expected. Attending key presentations for cultural awareness, safety, security and other important topics demonstrates their importance to the other members.

Oftentimes leaders receive a degree of latitude for deviations in training. Meaning, team members assume the leader is busy due to their role and responsibility. However, never underestimate the value of your presence participating in training. Not only does it allow you an opportunity to role model what is expected, it also provides additional time for you to bond, communicate and observe behavior and performance. Despite the latitude you receive as a leader, routinely missing mandatory "for everyone else" activities reflects poorly on you and degrades your influence. There will be critical elements of training and mission specific skills that cannot be left to chance. Therefore, participate in training and ensure you are using personal observations, reports and audits, also known as "leader checks," to "trust but verify" planned activities and standards are being adhered to. Also, ensure you not only participate to the fullest extent possible, but also document important aspects for accountability purposes.

Traveling to a mission location entails little effort by the leader unless he or she is actually driving or flying an aircraft, but the phase still requires diligence. Normally, deploying requires faith in the planning and confidence in your personnel to accomplish their roles. It is important to communicate the expectations to your people and to let them know they have autonomy and need to act without supervision to move the team. During the traveling phase, the leader's role is to encourage and be visible but to essentially let your people feel empowered to do their work.

The strengths and weaknesses of earlier planning will begin to unfold during movements. In many cases traveling may involve a lot of people moving from different locations along a time-phased schedule. Your people will quickly begin to recognize the effort put into the plan, or lack thereof, and may gain personal confidence in the leadership and the potential for success of the mission. In complex operations such as Natural Fire 10, recognize that with a convergence of people and equipment from all over the world, things will not go "smoothly." Therefore you must demonstrate patience and acceptance of the short-term dysfunction with confidence that it will all come together in brief order if people stay focused on their work.

Once team members have arrived at their destination they enter into the *staging* phase of an operation. Staging can be as simple as preparing medical supplies for distribution or as multifaceted as setting up remote basecamps to accommodate thousands of people and material. This is another period where people have been given their roles and your job is to provide a supportive environment and assist as necessary to ensure resources are being applied to meet the tasks. Whatever the complexity, the leaders' part is to participate in the effort and help wherever needed. People usually know what needs to be accomplished and you need to provide reassurance and support but not direct their work.

Conducting the mission is the reason you have made this trek and you serve a pivotal role in leading the effort. Realize that you cannot control everything that is going on and key aspects of the operation must be delegated to others. In complex operations with multiple activities commencing simultaneously, you have to empower team members to operate semi-autonomously. You physically cannot be everywhere at once so you must make decisions on where best to put yourself to add value. One method to prioritize both your time and your team's resources is to designate main, secondary and tertiary efforts for each part of your operation.

The main effort is often the most important or possibly the most dangerous task. It is also where you will position yourself to have the best opportunity to support the needs of your team by demonstrating moral support and ensuring the resources support their success onsite. Secondary and tertiary efforts are important but the entire mission may not hinge on their success. If you have other key leaders on your team they can be assigned to support the additional efforts. In addition to the leader's positioning for greatest effectiveness in an operation, the leader also serves as a "cheerleader-in-chief" internally by encouraging team members and externally by engaging with stakeholders and others who can assist the mission. The bottom line during this phase is you provide whatever is necessary to support your people and enable them to do their mission. Your role as a leader is to make them successful.

The *recovering* phase can be a challenge for leaders and team members. Transitions, especially in the military, are dangerous periods. This is the time that people take their eyes off the mission and start focusing their efforts at returning home. When an operations ends, the sense of purpose that kept people focused on the higher calling tends to subside and attention can quickly turn to self-orientation. Without leader involvement, your team may be basking in the accomplishments of the mission success one day and have violated a law, failed to take their medications, lost their passport or watch morale sink the next day. Leaders need to directly supervise recovery activities to ensure the attention given to the tasks necessary for mission completion are not overshadowed by the thoughts of moving on. A successful mission can be ruined by a hasty withdrawal and negative actions at the end.

Once you are in the *returning* phase you can take a breather and relax a little bit. This is essentially the travelling phase in reverse. Others are working on your behalf and your role as a leader is to encourage and be visible. Be diligent but let people feel empowered to do their work.

Upon returning to where you started, it's time to *refit*. Refit helps close the operation and set the stage for the next mission. This phase involves returning equipment, filing reports, paying bills and a host of other tasks necessary to officially close the mission. This is also the time to reflect and document the lessons learned so that others may benefit from the individual and collective experience and education that occurred. The leader must be very participative during this final operational period for a number of reasons. First, there is work to be done and oftentimes members will not be motivated to finish the administrative and other tasks now that the mission has been concluded. Second, the team needs psychological closure and the leaders' involvement will help move the group to adjournment. Finally, recognizing and rewarding behaviors sought and demonstrated through the operation sets expectations on performance standards for the next mission. Closing out your operation is akin to crossing the finish line of a race. As a leader, it is important to stay engaged with your people and push your team through completion.

Organizing work into phases provides organizational benefits such as: predictability, clarity of tasks, and efficiency. In addition to the value added by structuring work, planning a leadership strategy for each phase will help guide your effort to meet the needs of your people in each phase. As mentioned earlier, the U.S. military has numerous tools to guide the operational effort of leaders but they lack a coherent strategy to guide leadership behavior during various phases. One method I find valuable when considering the behaviors a leader should exhibit during an operation is to plan leadership engagement using the style approach.

The style approach to leadership is one of many methods to apply influence. The style approach is simple to understand and when used as a general azimuth to orient leader actions, can provide a start point to prepare yourself for the different phases of the mission. I want to stress I am not advocating a style approach as a comprehensive strategy to lead phases of a mission. There are circumstances and situations every day where a leader should change both their style and leadership approach based on the requirements of the situation and members abilities. However, that should not preclude you from preparing a strategy of engagement during an operation.

Table 5.1 provides the general orientation you should plan for during each phase of a mission. This is not prescriptive and instead a general orientation to prepare you for the challenges of each "chunk" of work. I have organized the table to correspond with both the four operational phases of work we planned for in Natural Fire 10 coupled with the sub-phases that serve as the core activities necessary to set the conditions for success.

A final thought for planning a leadership strategy for an operation – be consistent in your values, standards and ethics. While you may be routinely adjusting your leadership styles and influence

Table 5.1

Leadership Strategies during Operational Phases

Phase	Sub-phase	Style	Purpose	Things to Consider
Prede-ployment	Plan	Authorita-tive	A leader's direct involvement and decision are crit-ical for establish-ing confidence and ensuring the vision and intent of the mission are clear	Stay involved but don't micro-manage the process. Ensure you provide the right tone and avoid being bossy. Respect the people and their work.
	Prepare	Participa-tive	As preparation takes place, a supportive environment is necessary for people to make their unique contributions to the effort.	Demonstrate your adherence to standards and role model desired behavior.
	Train	Participa-tive	Leaders should be part of the team by demon-strating what is expected of the members and likelwise what they can expect from the leaders.	While followers provide lead-ers latitude for missing events, try not too.

(Continued)

strategies throughout your mission, people need your behaviors to be consistent. Research has shown that people prefer predictable leaders over unpredictable ones (even if *predictably bad*). The predictability they seek is through the behaviors borne from your principles. So while you adjust your style and influence to best fit the phases, situation and employee variables, ensure that you remain consistent with your standards.

Table 5.1 (continued)

Leadership Strategies during Operational Phases

Phase	Sub-phase	Style	Purpose	Things to Consider
Deploy-ment	Travel	Delegative	There is not much to control or influence. Be dependent on others.	Continue to communicate the vision, mission, and objective. Demonsrate patience.
	Stage	Participa-tive	You should assume the role of qunitessential team player.	Reassure people that their work is helping the mission and they are achieving standards. Ask how you can help.
Onsite Opera-tions	Conduct the Mission Stage	Delegative	Your people will realize their potential with your coaching. Trust, empower and check work. Be ready to assist and allocate resources.	You have to become the cheerleader-in-chief during mission execution. Your job is to be visible, supportive, and confident.

(Continued)

Table 5.1 (continued)

Leadership Strategies during Operational Phases

Phase	Sub-phase	Style	Purpose	Things to Consider
Redeployment	Recover	Authoritative	This is when people may let their guard down. Transitional periods are always dangerous and leaders need to get fully into the action.	It can be a shock to members when a leader suddenly seems to get interested in specific details following mission accomplishment. Stay involved even it is uncomfortable.
	Return	Delegative	Take a break on the flight home.	This is a good opportunity to hear more of the behind-the-scenes stories that occurred.
	Refit	Participative	The team needs you in a supportive role to help bring the mission to a successful close.	Reflect and document the accomplishments and lessons. Make sure to communicate to those that participated.

CHAPTER SIX

Building Your Team

With the deadline quickly approaching to deploy for Natural Fire 10, the 560th BFSB staff dove into the Phase I requirements of planning and preparation for the mission. We had already selected the Task Force Kitgum Headquarters Team using criteria including their specific military skills, demeanor, assignment in the brigade, diversity, potential for personal growth and leadership abilities. I was confident that the standards yielded a diverse group of people, with excellent skills they could contribute to the mission, and each would gain invaluable life and military experiences from their participation. Now we just had to get everyone quickly working as a high performance team.

The time constraints imposed for our participation in Natural Fire 10 mandated that normal team preparations, planning and training activities would be severely condensed. The entire pre-deployment process would be akin to the actions associated with crisis-action responses. The 24-members of our Task Force Kitgum team would have to move quickly through the stages of group development. As mentioned earlier, the value of building a team representative of the brigade, working them under the duress of time and forcing engagement and relationship building with a large group of decision makers and stakeholders may have initially been lost on participants. However, these same challenges would prove to be excellent preparatory drills to equip the group with interpersonal skills they would soon apply on the ground.

Before embarking on specific protocols for team building

with the group, I introduced a set of leader strategies to the team to help them understand the psychosocial dynamics of group performance and prepare accordingly. This information was not only to set the conditions for our pre-mission team development but also prepare the group for their future requirements in Uganda. In Kitgum they would be expected to assimilate a diverse group of joint forces and multiple nations' military personnel; a group numbering over 1,000 personnel. Being knowledgeable about and exposed to group dynamic principles and activities would both enhance our maturity as a team in the days ahead as well as prepare the personnel for their role executing similar strategies in Uganda.

There were several structured activities that helped with the group's development during this short period. We set a schedule of educational activities to provide participants broad themes associated with principles, concepts and values that encouraged communications, discussion and collective learning. We trained on predictable tasks and scenarios expected to occur during the mission to give each person confidence in their individual skills and those of their teammates. Finally, we conducted administrative tasks together designed to both prepare the personnel for the mission and bring them together as a team. People internal to the group were chosen to lead the educational, training and administrative aspects of the mission. The purposeful selections offered each member an opportunity to influence the group and enabled them to demonstrate competency to team.

One of the Soldiers was a sergeant who grew up in Kenya and spoke Swahili. Naturally she was identified to teach the group some basic expressions in Swahili that we practiced together. She also was instrumental for providing cultural awareness of many aspects of dealing with people in East Africa. Our intelligence personnel were tasked to provide historical, political, and military background information to participants. We educated ourselves on cultural communications and the nuances of working in Uganda, the local Acholi people we would interface with in Kitgum, and our African partners. Between the formal classes, personal study and discourse among the group, a collective understanding of the region and its people emerged to guide our planning, interactions and operational decisions on the ground in Kitgum.

We had selected a medical services officer to accompany our team and he provided our extensive medical education. The captain did a superb job providing hygiene and health classes on the seemingly endless disease threats including EVD, Plague, Malaria, Yellow fever, Dengue fever, Marburg fever, Rabies, Schistosomiasis, Diarrheic diseases, HIV, Meningitis, Tuberculosis, Cholera, Diptheria, Hepatitis A & B, Tetanus, Typhoid, and Poliomyelitis. The captain took great pride in finding the most grotesque pictures of advanced stages of the various diseases as well as noting that Uganda had one of the longest lists of diseases according to the Centers for Disease Control (CDC). The health instruction made a convincing case and motivated our participants to attend all scheduled immunizations and complete full dosage amounts – which we conducted as a group under the captain's supervision. These events included both shots and oral doses at various points. In each case, as the appointed leader I received the first shot or dose of immunization and each person followed in turn. Each of these periods, were considered an opportunity to demonstrate taking the correct action, our resolve to one another, our willingness to endure for mission and to lead by example.

For training, we drew the special gear we would use in Uganda and together practiced the steps necessary to place our equipment into operation and remedy potential dysfunction. Our Task Force Kitgum communications section conducted formal training classes and drills to operate Single Channel Ground Air Radio System (SINGCARS), High Frequency (HF) radio systems, Single Channel (S/C) Tactical Satellite (TACSAT), satellite phones and other items. The medical officer transitioned from educating us on the threats to training us on basic first aid procedures including the usage of first aid and trauma kits. All of our training tasks were conducted together to assist in our group development. The sessions provided structure, offered opportunities to communicate amongst each other and built a foundation of basic skills that each person knew we would need for the mission.

One of the most significant team building events we conducted collectively was counter-terrorism training. Through our security briefings and mission analysis, we knew of multiple threats posed by potential terrorists or criminal threats in Uganda. We also recognized our most vulnerable periods were going to be during transitions and in movements. This would particularly be true on contract busses where we may not have a security escort or access to protection.

On September 15, 2009, we assembled the Natural Fire 10 team at our headquarters building on Fort Gillem for several days of hand-to-hand fighting skills. The group was somewhat apprehensive about spending the next few days conducting combatives but the threats to the team were real and so would be our training. Our instructor, a renown mixed martial arts expert in Haganah, was a very imposing and charismatic figure. Haganah is a reality-fighting program and direct descendent of the Krav Maga system developed by the Israeli Defense Forces (IDF). Haganah combines skills from boxing, wrestling, jiu-jitsu, judo, and grappling as well as a few other fighting styles. The instructor masterfully walked each member through various techniques to disarm and neutralize threats without weapons. Full participation was expected by the instructor and anything less earned the opportunity for you to become the demonstrator, his adversary, at each step in the training – ouch.

By the end of the first day, we were beginning to realize proficiency with several of the moves and understood the basics of protection and defensive postures for various vehicles. We knew the likely access for a terrorist onto a bus, where to position our personnel in seats close to the entrances, how to respond quickly to armed and unarmed threats and of course became very knowledgeable with the

82

penalty for not giving full participation! This was serious training and our instructor was a serious man.

On the second day, our instructor moved us from the simulated environments in the building out to actual busses to add realism to the training. I had never realized how difficult it was to maneuver on a bus or how important it was to quickly collapse an opponent onto the floor where they have almost no ability to fight back due to the restricted conditions of the seats and support struts. We spent the day fighting in the cramped conditions of different types of busses against adversaries armed with knives, pistols, rifles and Improvised Explosive Devices (IEDs). We lunged over seats to control the hands holding potential IED triggers, and stripped away various weapons from potential threats with force and confidence. By the end of the second day of training everyone was bruised and beat up. The bus took a beating as well with a broken mirror and windshield, evidence of the realism in the training and rehearsals. Despite our minor physical injuries, psychologically we were confident that any of our members could effectively remove a threat to the group.

Fighting on a bus was one of several structured events designed to both acquire skills for the upcoming mission and also advance our group development. Each of the activities aided our group's maturation by providing a deliberate process for communicating and learning about our team members. The combatives training in particular served its purpose from both a task perspective as well as from a psychological perspective by placing all members of the group in a physically and mentally challenging activity together. Fighting on a bus, while a seemingly bizarre method, was one of many techniques to unify the team. We would employ similar strategies on the ground in Uganda to bring the entire Task Force together.

Leader Strategies for Building a Team

Constructing a high performance team normally takes a pe

Table 6.1

Building Your Team

Order	Key Terms	Leader Strategy
1	Adhocracy	Recognize you are likely working in adhocracy and the challenges associated with accelerated or restricted timelines.
2	The Right People	Request or allocate educated, experienced and influential members from the agencies participating in crisis planning.
3	Stages of Group Development	Understand and prepare for the general psychosocial dynamics of group maturation - have a plan to provide structure for the team but prepare to deviate as necessary to enhance effectiveness.
4	Relationships	Know that relationships are paramount to multinational and interagency success – devote time and resources to this critical element.

riod of time devoted to develop people to particular quality. Unfortunately, many leaders find themselves in situations where they are expected to build a team and respond to an event where time is not an abundant resource. This section is designed to provide you with strategies to build a team during challenging periods including crisis events. To effectively lead you have to recognize the environment you will be working in, pick the right people, develop the group, provide structure, and build relationships. These seemingly simple tasks require a strategy for success. Table 6.1 displays four leadership strategies you should embrace to effectively build a team in a time-constrained environment or crisis event.

There is one universal lesson that I have learned from leading diverse operations - each mission is unique. For the 560th BFSB, Natural Fire 10 represented a completely new challenge, in an unfamiliar environment, and with a plethora of variables that we had not previously prepared for. Despite our leadership role we did not have the time, were without formal control over the mission's assets, had not met key participants, and yet still responsible for attaining results in the operation. Our normal standard operating procedures and time-lines did not apply to Natural Fire 10 and our preparations were akin to crisis action planning. Sometimes just recognizing you are dealing with a crisis is helpful for determining your response as a leader.

A *crisis* is characterized by the failure of a complex system, or a sequence of events expected or with the potential to lead to a dangerous or unstable situation. The term is often used synonymously with *emergencies* despite a significant difference for leaders. You will often have to *lead* a crisis while you can *manage* an emergency.

An *emergency* is a predictable scenario for which you are organized, equipped, and trained to handle. Emergencies are even scalable, meaning they have predictable plug-ins to mitigate the situation that are rehearsed and often called upon. A good example of a scalable emergency situation is when a fire department responds to burning building. The first fire crew will begin the process of response and if it is beyond its capabilities another crew will be called. That process continues to include additional alarms (commitment of additional resources) and their capabilities resulting in a scaled capacity to mitigate the emergency.

Recall for a moment the situation at the World Trade Centers (WTC's) during the terrorist attack on 911. When hijackers crashed American Airlines Flight 11 into the 1 WTC at 9:03 a.m. the local New York emergency response force jumped into action responding to the burning building. As the Fire Department of New York, New York Police Department and other agencies exercised their emergency response protocols, United Airlines Flight 175 crashed into the 2 WTC at 9:37 a.m. Additional responders poured into the area to scale appropriately to the situation. Emergency responders evacuated the buildings, set up triage centers to deal with injured personnel, cleared streets and set up a command post to run the operation. Then at 9:59 a.m. 1 WTC collapsed followed by 2 WTC at 10:28 a.m. The situation went from an emergency to a crisis as over 2,606 people perished including 340 firefighters, 60 law enforcement officers, and the entire consequence management headquarters and leadership.

During 911 the situation suddenly and unexpectedly moved from a manageable response to an event where the collective capacity of the response infrastructure was completely overwhelmed. The entire situation, using planes as IED's, and the resultant catastrophic consequences are considered a *novelty* for response planners (Howitt & Leonard, 2009). A novelty in crises events refers to the unconventional nature, unfamiliar processes, and unusual characteristics of the incident. Novel events typically require adaptation and organizational transformation.

Despite directives, doctrine and experiences, there does not appear to be a best prescription for organizing diverse occurrences. The U.S. government, particularly the military, spends inordinate energy preparing plans and after action reviews (AARs) to provide "go to" documents for leaders and planners to use to help guide their efforts. Unfortunately they routinely fail to review these plans to avoid reinventing and relearning previous lessons and instead have them sit on shelves during crisis events dooming the participants to many of the same mistakes made in previous incidences. Often compounding the problems, in almost all cases we organize differently for each situation. This is completely understandable in that each situation is completely unique, requiring a range of options and resources specific to the environment and the actors involved. The common practice for U.S. agencies, at all levels, is to routinely organize in an improvised fashion. When a response involves other countries, or accommodates new players, organizations, resources, and other variables to accomplish the mission you will almost certainly find yourself in an ad hoc configuration.

Adhocracy.

Ad hoc (Latin meaning "for this") refers to an organizational solution, created under special circumstances, for a specific task, and not intended to be adapted for other purposes. Crisis events often require leaders to construct new organizations based on the situation, their immediate needs, the environment, and various response entities (the people involved). Probably the best phrase to capture the organizing philosophy for an improvised response is *adhocracy*. Adhocracy was coined by Mintzberg and McHugh (1985) and referred to a project group that met the following characteristics:

> (1) The organization operates in an environment that is both dynamic and complex, demanding innovation of a fairly sophisticated nature. Each output tends to be unique.
> (2) The production of complex, unique outputs forces the organization to engage highly trained experts and combine their talents in multidisciplinary teams.
> (3) These experts are housed in specialized units for administrative and housekeeping purposes, but are deployed in temporary teams to work on their projects.
> (4) Because of the complex and unpredictable nature of its work, the organization relies largely on mutual adjustment and coordination, which is encouraged by semiformal structural parameters such as liaison personnel and standing committees.
> (5) The organization is decentralized "selectively": power over different decisions is diffused in uneven ways (p160-161).

Interestingly, the paradigm of the U.S. and other nations differs significantly regarding organizing during a crisis. The U.S. perspective on organization follows the assumption that if the right structure is built first, then whoever is assigned to lead the mission will be successful. On the other hand, many Europeans including the British, believe you must find the right person first, and then build a structure around that individual to have a better outcome. The question then becomes: get the right structure or get the right person?

With history as a guide, one can assume a novel event will

require an adaptation to your organization. The designated leader will have the most impact regarding structuring the team and an ad hoc configuration will likely emerge. Keep in mind that whatever your ad hoc configuration, the organizational design should enhance the qualities, qualifications and abilities of the people. If the structure does not support the people it will fail the organization. Your adhocracy should be "living," and ought to evolve to support the skills and abilities of the people you bring to the team.

The Right People.

It is not surprising that when it comes to assembling a team, *"Getting the right people"* is one of the foremost recommendations from the research. Failure to include the correct parties in the interagency planning process is widely known for adversely impacting the mission through incongruent action and inadequate resource optimization (Hollen, Mundell, Nison, & Sweeney, 2003). The selection of individual participants impacts both the ability of the crisis planning team to accomplish its tasks and the quality of the group's outputs. Success is often the result of a *cross functional* (also referred to as a multidisciplinary) arrangement of *diverse* expertise and resources (Beers, Boshuizen, Kirshner, & Gijselaers, 2006; Peelle, 2006). Leaders must attempt to select a team whose members have a combination of specific job skills as well as the ability to reach back with decision making authority to their home organizations for support of the team's work.

There are two perspectives for identifying diversity that leaders ought to acquire for their teams. *Functional diversity* is job related expertise and the different viewpoints brought to complex organizational decisions. *Positional diversity* is another job-related attribute based on formal titles and the underlying skills assumed from tenure and experience. *Positional diversity* is a more important factor for team performance in that lower level members of organizational hierarchy may contribute opinions while higher level members can provide both experience and exercise influence in decision making (Yeh & Chu, 2005).

The value of positional diversity for cross-functional team performance is well documented. For instance, during past congressional testimony regarding interagency effectiveness, it was recommended that agency executives carefully identify experts in regional and functional offices to serve on interagency crisis planning teams to assist in achieving unity of effort (Flournoy, 2008). These experts with their respective influence and reach-back capability could truly develop interagency campaign plans with combatant command planners. While positional elements may be more important for team performance, most researchers agree that effective planning cannot occur without functional experts to provide advice and guidance (Peelle, 2006). United Nations planning teams chartered to provide support in Liberia, Sudan, Haiti, and Iraq specifically invited NGO's and members of civil society based on their expertise to address planning effectiveness (United Nations, 2006). While invitations to participate can provide some level of support to crisis planning, experience shows that it is imperative to include, not just invite the right participants.

As you form your crisis-leadership group, attempt to solicit those with both seniority in their parent organization and practical experience. Oftentimes in multinational operations you may not be able to select people for their functional or positional diversity. As a matter of fact, you are likely to receive or inherit whoever has been provided, and in some cases they may be volunteers. When that happens your challenge will be to identify their skills and expertise and arrange in a way that best enables their talents to contribute to the operation from a positional or functional diversity perspective. Keep in mind that selection of the "right people" will improve group performance, hasten plan production and enhance execution of supporting actions during a crisis. Make every effort to communicate and ask for what will best serve the mission.

Stages of Group Development.

Once the people are selected for your team you cannot expect that you will suddenly be able to produce results. Instead your team will move through several steps on a path to high performance (Montebello & Buzzotta, 1993). Tuckmen and Jenson (1977) described a psychosocial process of group development to generalize changes in a group's life over time. They found two realms of human interaction, task interactions and interpersonal interactions, which appeared to best characterize the interface among team members moving through group development. The interpersonal realm referred to the interactions that occurred among members related to structure, while the task realm dealt with exchanges between people related to the team's task requirements. For example, when our team was fighting on a bus, there were interpersonal realm interactions that occurred due to the schedule of events, organization of people into practice groups, and general hierarchy of authority. When two people paired up to practice a specific task such as disarming an attacker with a pistol, the task realm interactions that occurred while they talked and walked through the steps to mitigate the threat were an example of a task interaction.

Tuckmen and Jenson (1977) summarized the task-interpersonal groupings into four stages of group development referred to as "forming, storming, norming, performing" and added later the additional stage of "adjourning" (p. 420). It is important to note the first two stages –"forming and storming" - pose the greatest challenges to leaders assembling a team in a time-constrained environment.

Forming.

When a team is assembled, the first phase of group development is known as the "*forming*" stage. The forming stage is related to testing and orientation to the team's task requirements. A simple but important component of the forming stage is for the team members to be present. The accessibility of personnel from different organizations is not always convenient for interagency or multinational arrangements. When you do not "own" the personnel all you can do is ask designated organizations for the right participants and for specific arrival time. Unfortunately, this challenge is not easily overcome. The United Nations has routinely identified the dysfunction that occurs when participants arrive at different stages or late into the planning process (United Nations, 2006).

Requesting the right people has already been identified as an important strategy for developing functional and positional diversity into your team. An additional step to requesting the right people is also calling for background information from the host agency. During the forming phase, a leader's knowledge of team participants can greatly assist in the alignment of skills and talents to tasks. Knowing who is participating on your team will enable you to arrange assignments in a manner with the greatest potential for decision-making and coordination. For instance, if you are to receive a Kenyan officer to work in your operations center and you know he has experience in transportation and support, assigning him to work with logistics (in the military logistics includes transportation and support) will likely yield efficiency in his personal output. Even if a person arrives to the group with little expertise for a specific team requirement, knowledge of the individual's experience or seniority can provide an opportunity to position that individual for team performance.

During the forming stage, it is common for team members to have anxiety regarding their new assignment, fear regarding their role, and a lack of trust with other group members (Montebello & Buzzotta, 1993). Leaders can assist members during this phase by planning social interactions, taking emphasis off the task, and creating predictability by explaining the processes the group will be using to work together (Henderson-Loney, 1996). Leaders must be cognizant of the indicators of distress such as anger, withdrawal and resistance as they hinder group development. However, equally important is to recognize that eustress is healthy and provides the potential for high performance among individuals. A paradox exists as supervisors will often stereotype stress into a negative psycho-physiological context while individual stress responses are known to be an innate asset for achieving peak performance (Quick, Quick, Nelson, & Hurrell, 1997).

An important process of the forming stage is *rapport* building among members. Rapport essentially means "sameness" and rapport-building is critical for psychologically connecting the group members. Finding commonality builds teamwork. After-action reviews from operations in Bosnia and Kosovo noted that developing solid personal relationships was a critical element of mission success (Hollen et al., 2003).

The value of people and their relationships in multinational, multicultural, multiagency, and multi-jurisdictional operations cannot be overstated. Most of your team will be derived from a myriad of organizations with various agendas, political considerations, policies and other potential barriers that can hinder or stop progress towards your mission objectives. Relationships are the most important element you can foster to reduce the potential for organizational inertia and best articulated by Gibbons, Hurley and Moore, (1998): "Individuals breathe life into the bureaucratic process. They may enable workarounds to meet a common goal, to enhance their feelings of power, or to cope when they conclude that the stakes warrant non-standard behavior" (p. 103).

Storming.

While relationships are an important starting point for group development, you are dealing with people and their varied beliefs, experiences, and emotions and as a leader you can expect some friction to occur. The "*storming*" stage occurs as the group struggles with its identity. Storming (to stir) refers to a disturbance in the group atmosphere. The group will move to an agitated state due to conflict from the assignment or self-selection of roles and responsibilities. The drive of the group is to evolve structure and boundaries (Bass, 1990). This period provides a challenge for leaders regarding organization (*command and control*) and *sense-making*. Rationality, predictability and ambiguity reduction are hallmarks of the command and control mental model and akin to a machine-like approach to structuring the group. A bureaucratic scheme will facilitate role assignments but ultimately may limit the ability of members to contribute at their potential.

On the other hand, sense-making is an interpretive group process that seeks to allow participants to assign meaning and gain a better understanding of the uncertainties they face together (Ashmos & Nathan, 2002). Several researchers have argued that group members must first search for a common frame of reference to bridge differences before they can contribute their skills and experience to the address problems (Beers et al., 2006). Leader emphasis should be on human relationships and good communication to improve the speed with which knowledge is created among members (Breen, Fetzer, Howard, & Previosi, 2005).

While leader facilitation is critical for moving the group through the storming stage, not all techniques provide for constructive or sustainable cooperation. In a multinational context, leaders must recognize that common American theories of motivation, leadership and organization may not accelerate this critical stage of group development. Hofstede (1980) also concluded the "consequences of the cultural relativity of management theories are more serious for the multinational organization" (p.62). Hofstede (1980) noted that management theories typically worked best within the culture in which they were developed. An important implication for leaders is to recognize the different perspectives and underlying assumptions associated with the cultures represented in the group. Joint Publications 3-16 (2013) aptly prescribed respect, rapport, knowledge of partners, patience, mission focus and trust as tenets for unity of effort among members.

While it is common to view conflict as negative, research has shown that suppressing conflict may reduce creativity, innovation, decision quality and ultimately the team's performance (Medina, Lourdes, Dorado, Martinenez, & Guerra, 2005). *Task* and *relational conflict* are two types of intra-group conflict with different personal and organizational consequences. *Task conflict* is associated with the distribution of resources, procedures, and interpretation of facts and often results in innovation and increase of constructive debate. On the other hand, *relational conflict* involves disagreements regarding values and personal elements that negatively affect a member's satisfaction, tension and commitment to the group. Discord within the storming phase must be anticipated and understood by the supervisor but neither task nor relational friction should be suppressed (Medina et al, 2005).

Norming.

Once the conflict and bargaining have ended, members begin to explore their new roles, identify with the group and work at the tasks assigned. This "*norming*" of behavior and organizational processes creates an environment where the team can successfully complete tasks and its mission. The group operates to develop cohesiveness in this phase with roles accepted, and communication and trust improved (Bass, 1990). Leaders should take a relations-oriented approach and facilitate, always cognizant of unresolved issues that may impact the production and continued development of the group (Henderson-Loney, 1996).

94

Performing.

The fourth phase occurs as mutual commitment, internal structuring, open communications, and removal of obstacles create an environment for performance. The "*performing*" stage of development is when the group becomes a team with a shared sense of purpose and direction, and the motivation to act. An important concept during the performing stage is adjustment. Much like a professional sports team after you've completed practices, as the environment and requirements are changing you must adjust your team to achieve optimum performance. It is common for groups to continue to develop, adjust and re-form during the performing phase. While the re-forming does not typically involve changes in the interpersonal dynamics previously established in the "forming" and "storming" stages, it does address re-evaluation of goals, evaluating progress to date, and revising plans in order to refocus their effort to complete task requirements (Bass, 1990). To use a football analogy, your team may not be able to advance 10 yards a play so you adjust your goal to 5 yards based on the external and internal changes occurring during game performance.

Adjourning.

The final stage of group development is the process of "*adjourning.*" Groups, particularly those formed to address specific projects such as crisis planning teams, will likely terminate following their mission and experience some level of adjournment from their ad hoc arrangements. Whether the entire group returns to parent organizations or selected experts leave the team, closure is an important psychosocial component. The process of group maturation, particularly under duress, forms unique bonds among participants. Closure is very difficult for many people and you want to ensure that team members can say "we accomplished this," "good work," "if you ever need help again…" "thank you," and "goodbye." Leaders can address closure by formally concluding the group's mission, reviewing processes and actions, recognizing individual and collective contributions, and ensuring personal relationships are left intact.

Tuckman and Jensen's (1977) five stages of group development provide a pragmatic lens for leaders to plan and prepare for the challenges of crisis action planning in adhocracy. Several researchers have concluded that effective leadership facilitates the process of group development and systematically moves the group to maturation and performance (Bass, 1990). Others note human behavior is not linear and individuals move in and out of the phases at different paces. Leaders knowledgeable in group-dynamics can predict the process and prepare members by reassuring them that the experience they are having is normal (Henderson-Loney, 1996).

Keeping a "One team, one fight" mentality and unity of effort are keys to successful crisis operations (Luck & Findlay, 2008). The complexity of today's environment is such that most, if not all, crisis planning events will involve two or more countries, agencies or non-governmental organizations. Department of Defense Joint Publication 3-16 (2013) provides some useful advice for conducting multinational operations. In conjunction with Joint Publication 3-16 (2013), the four leadership strategies of *recognizing adhocracy, finding the right people, understanding and preparing for group development* and *focusing on relationships* can assist leaders to integrate the right members and work quickly through the early stages of group maturation. The end result is improved performance and production of coordinated and synchronized plans for crisis mitigation.

CHAPTER SEVEN

Structuring Your Organization

In order to properly structure our Task Force Kitgum we first had to understand our portion of the Natural Fire 10 mission. What were the mission requirements and what are we required to do? Only after a thorough mission analysis whereby you clearly understand your functions and objectives can you develop a mechanism to help organize and accomplish your goals. Your organizational structure serves as the instrumentality for achieving your objectives.

The Natural Fire 10 exercise was the culmination of over a year of planning among interagency and multinational representatives. Formal arrangements were made at the macro level at conferences and coordinating meetings regarding country-to-country treaties, contracting, resources, scheduling, logistics, medical support, training plans and a host of other items (VanAmburgh, 2011). There was a slight opportunity for potential Task Force members to learn about one another beforehand but the majority of the actual participants would meet for the first time in Kitgum when the operation commenced. This meant that the people actually running the activities of Natural Fire 10 would not have the opportunity to build a structure for the mission until all had assembled. Instead we had to devise a structure that could be implemented immediately and both serve the mission and the Task Force participants. From the outset, we could surmise the Task Force would require a structure characterized by:

(1) Innovation – we had people from six different countries with a significant amount of expertise and experience and we needed to be able capitalize on their ideas and change our structure as necessary to meet new challenges;

(2) Unique outputs – our force was being assembled for a specific set of requirements associated with Natural Fire 10. The Task Force would need to be able to produce the results specific to the requirements;

(3) Temporary arrangement of people and resources – each country would send in their people and assets for the mission and quickly withdraw once the operation was concluded; and

(4) Influence largely reliant upon mutual adjustment and coordination – our Task Force was comprised of foreign forces participating through an agreement. As the commander, I did not have formal command over any elements other than the U.S. component. We had to rely on the spirit of partnership and adjust for each other's strengths and weaknesses toward common objectives.

One of the greatest leadership failures often made preparing and planning for a mission is in developing the organizational structure. Most people, particularly Americans, are very quick to try and develop a line and block hierarchal chart to depict relationships without first determining what truly needs to be accomplished. Instead, remember the phrase, *"Form follows function."* This simple expression will keep you from inadvertently making the number one organizational mistake when planning. First, determine your required *functions* and *then* build your organizational structure (*form*) to support those efforts.

As mentioned earlier, the organizing assumption in the U.S. is that if you get the structure right, you can put almost anyone into the designated leadership roles and be successful. Contrasting that model, the British employ an organizing strategy of identifying the individuals who are going to lead the effort and build the structure to support the strengths and weaknesses of the people in relation to the mission. The best approach is to determine the functions required, identify the "right" people for the leader roles, and then design your structure accordingly. Make every effort to avoid the "structure first" conundrum and you will have missed a classic and common error that yields large negative consequences.

Two overarching objectives identified by AFRICOM helped drive the organizing strategy for the coalition force in Natural Fire 10: (1) build relationships, and (2) enhance the capabilities of our partner nations. That meant that when the operation concluded our results had to consist of international level unity between the U.S. and the East African nations, personal relationships among the participants, and trained cadre from each organization who could bring back the experience and enhance their country's capabilities. The cadre should be versed in the various activities being undertaken by the Task Force including command and control, communications, security, humanitarian assistance including medical and dental triage and care, reconstruction, and logistics.

In addition to AFRICOM's objectives, we also had to produce results and succeed in our ability to project power, provide humanitarian assistance, and secure our force. Subsequently, Task Force Kitgum faced four major organizational challenges: (1) assembling people with the right skills and knowledge; (2) exercising influence over participants without being able to rely on formal controls; (3) balancing the administrative need for efficiency and economy with the requirement for responsiveness and (4) building community among the participants. The totality of requirements necessitated an organizing strategy that combined engagement with execution. Engagement refered to our ability to build commitment and involvement with all the parties involved, and execution denoted our competence to complete the mission to the fullest extent.

Through our mission analysis we determined that Task Force

Kitgum would need to effectively direct the activities of the Task Force, protect our members, execute medical, dental and engineer operations, and house, feed, fuel, maintain, and generally sustain our people and equipment. These were the most important functions of the Task Force because failure in any one functional area could have jeopardized the operation. For instance, without command you could expect coordination problems, failing to secure our force could mean the medical and engineer personnel could not treat people or repair/construct buildings, and if we ran out of food, fuel or shelter the operation would cease to continue. We concluded the four main functional areas of Task Force Kitgum would be *command and control, security, humanitarian assistance,* and *support.*

The command and control function would be executed by the Task Force headquarters through the various entities allocated to the organization. The headquarters was predominately staffed by the 560th BFSB and augmented by African personnel. The 560th BFSB would be the "owner" of the command and control function. We identified that security functions were predominately a U.S. Marine requirement and subsequently assigned them ownership of that functional areas. The humanitarian assistance mission had been previously coordinated by civil affairs who would best be the owner of all medical, dental and engineer personnel to support this function. The general logistics necessary to sustain the force such as feeding and fresh water, fuel, contracting, and a host of other activities was the support function and belonged to a U.S. Army support battalion imported from Germany. They would be charged with sustaining the force and running the basecamp operation.

The grouping of employees to broad business activites is comonly referred to as a *functional organizational structure*. The functional organizational structure creates efficiency and specialization but it can also become rigid and bureaucratic over time. When people are grouped together with similar skills, their in-depth knowledge can be focused on meeting functional goals. Subsequently specialization can emerge leading to enhanced productivity. On the other hand, restricted views can impact the ability of employees to innovate and communicate with other functional areas. We needed to create a structure that would support productivity and be responsive to changing conditions with the ability to evolve quickly.

As such, we clarified the functions and alignment with organizational owners so we could also identify a designated leader who could be both empowered and accountable for the processes being conducted within that area. The assignment of ownership to a functional area and associated processes is called *process-ownership* and will be covered in a successive chapter. While our organizational structure was based on functions it was applied using a *process ownership model*. Functional organization can be an effective method for organizing as long as you fully enable and empower the owner to complete the process they are accountable for. For example, the U.S. Marines owned the majority of the military police, weapons, vehicles and security expertise making them not only the owner of the function but also the owner of the resources necessary for the processes to be completed. Had we removed the vehicles from the Marines they would not have had the assets to be able to carry out there function and any success or failure could not be directly attributed to their efforts. Instead, the Marines were trained, equipped and empowered to provide security throughout the mission and could be accountable to Task Force for the security functional area.

In order to address the challenge of relations and involvement, we established an *integrated command structure*. This form was chosen to fully incorporate partner nation personnel into the command. The integrated command structure merges or augments coordinating staff elements together to provide unity of effort among the participants. For Natural Fire 10, I was named as the formal commander with the 560th BFSB team serving as the staff primaries of the Task Force Kitgum coordinating staff (S1 – administration, S2 – intelligence, S3 – Operations, and S4 – logistics). The Task Force deputy commander role was reserved for a Ugandan Lieutenant Colonel who also commanded the local Ugandan security force in the area around Kitgum. To round out the coordinating staff positions in Task Force Kitgum, personnel were identified and sent over from each of the other African countries participating. These people served to both represent their countries and also be a counterpart to each U.S. member of the coordinating staff to partner in the command of the Task Force and its units.

English was chosen as the common language among the command and staff. One of the first steps to opening communications is to establish a common language. As simple as that may seem, when you are dealing with multiple countries a common language has varying degrees of comprehension, accents and ability levels by the participants. When you have different agencies, jurisdictions or other entities, their understanding of acronyms, terminology and other elements could cloud understanding and result in miscommunication and organizational dysfunction. In some cases a common language can have interesting and unintended results like one interaction between a Kenyan officer and a U.S. Soldier writing a report. The Kenyan stood over his shoulder and spent considerable time correcting the U.S. Soldier's improper English.

Most work production requires some degree of communication with others. This is especially true of organizations that have not had the opportunity to mature communications through internal problem solving or externally driven adaptation. When procedures and systems are not mature or sophisticated, good old-fashioned word-of-mouth is the primary means to pass information. In a complex multinational operation it is not just a simple passing of information that is required, members need to communicate in order to collaborate and accomplish their mission requirements.

The common lesson that often emerges during complex multinational operations is that relationships will sustain the mission. When bureaucratic structures and systems fail, the people and their

Figure 7.1. Combatives training on the basecamp. The Marines masterfully integrated with African forces to create multinational teams within Task Force Kitgum. Photo by Sandra Smith.

established relationships can break down barriers, overcome obstacles and find a way to make the mission succeed (VanAmburgh, 2011). Since the Task Force leadership team had previous experience and knowledge in multinational operations and also understanding of the psycho-social aspects of group development (for example, storming, norming, etc… from previous reading) we ensured relationship-building was a priority from the start. Careful arrangement of personnel, the physical design and flow of the headquarters facility into tabletop cells to encourage crosstalk, coupled with official and unofficial social engagements were all employed to assist in relationship and team building.

Aside from the integrated command structure employed in the Task Force headquarters, opening communications among the coalition troops was another challenge particularly since a common language was not as easily chosen below the command level. At echelons hierarchically under the headquarters, Task Force teams had to work through English, Swahili and French. Despite the language barriers we took a similar integrated approach that comingled all countries during the daily activities. The security force was a perfect example of this approach in action.

As previously identified by our process ownership organizational model, the U.S. Marines were in charge of actual security and security training activities across the Task Force enterprise. Subsequently, forces were allocated from each of the partner nations to participate in the security functions. The security force was organized into platoon-sized groups of 30-40 soldiers representing each of the six countries participating in Natural Fire 10. The efficient choice would have been to organize the platoons by country to take advantage of common language, chain of command, common equipment and tactics. However, instead of building a security platoon from Burundi, another from Kenya, and so as each country had an organic platoon, we integrated each platoon with personnel from each of the participating nations. Every country was represented in every platoon. This strategy was designed to ensure unity of effort not just a theme resident among the high-ranking personnel in the Task Force, but was experienced by every member of the coalition.

In addition to the integration at the soldier level, each of the platoons had a different country senior sergeant as the leader. Although we may have been able to create efficiencies by organizing the force along national lines, we would have missed the greater opportunity of forming relationships, interdependency and growth. We chose to build multinational teams, not just conduct a multinational operation. None of the Task Force functions (command & control, security, humanitarian assistance, and logistics) or their sub-elements were broken out by country and instead staffed as a coalition effort along functional lines. After overcoming initial language and group formation issues, teams quickly matured and worked in a cooperative-competitive environment amongst their peers. In the evenings after the day's tasks were completed, the participants would reside in their respective encampments but during the operations it was a completely multinational approach. Our organizing and integrating strategy would serve us well throughout Natural Fire 10.

When structuring your organization remember that form follows function. First, establish what you are here to do (purpose and functions) by a thorough mission analysis, *then* determine how you are going to do it. The structure should support your functions and key processes. I admit to being an advocate of process-ownership as a model for organizational design. Assigning ownership allows for accountability if you ensure that your owners have access to the resources and are empowered to make decisions concerning their processes. This structure worked well for Natural Fire 10 when coupled with the integration strategy employed throughout Task Force Kitgum. The value of integrating all the participants in multinational teams cannot be overstated. It enhances unity of effort across the force and mitigates the potential for country-level elements to become isolated in the mission.

SECTION THREE

Building a Coalition

CHAPTER EIGHT

A Little Faith

The operation in Kitgum was heavily influenced by an uncontrollable element, good weather. Uganda enjoys a tropical climate and the country's weather depends on the geographic location. Temperature ranges from 85 degrees during the day to 60 degrees at night. The country has two dry seasons from December to February and June to August. For planning purposes the rainy season lasts from March to May and the country encounters light rain from November to December. The city of Kitgum is located in northern Uganda and is typically a little dryer than the central or southern portions of the country. Central and southern Uganda's atmospheric conditions are influenced by Lake Victoria and moist southwesterly winds emanating from the neighboring Democratic Republic of Congo result in routine rain and thunderstorms. Frequent, heavy thunderstorms last from 30 minutes to one hour and in the rainy season although it seldom rains the entire day. The optimum period to conduct Natural Fire 10 appeared to be in the September-October timeframe coming off the dry season but prior to the start of the rainy season. It was expected that Natural Fire 10 participants would encounter Uganda's typical bright and sunny days during the preparation, execution and closing of the mission.

Unfortunately, bright and sunny days were not to be found in the preparation stage of Natural Fire 10. During the weeks leading up to the operation, heavy rains moved into the Kitgum area and would not seem to let up. Uganda is covered in Red Murram dust that can be a particular problem throughout the year. In the dry season,

109

the dust never seems to settle with clouds of the fine material visible around any trafficked area. During the rains, the dust turns into a fine and slippery red mud. For those who have spent time in Georgia or Alabama, think of red clay and how slick it can be if you get a vehicle mired in the soupy mess. In Kitgum, the mud and standing water hindered all movement into the area other than by foot traffic. Despite the hard working nature of the Acholi people in the region, the portage of enough building materials to construct a basecamp for over 1,000 people was just not feasible. The contractor, a local expatriate from South Africa, was quite literally stuck at a certain point in the construction and could not proceed.

While the planning continued in the U.S. and Europe the basecamp site was a mess. The area started out covered in low brush and tall grass in the center of a small UPDF encampment. Heavy equipment bulldozed the field exposing the Red Murram to the heavy rains. The resultant muck was like a sludge pit where each step sucked your feet into six inches of mud. Even the Ugandan soldiers in area stayed clear of this eyesore programmed to be the future home of Task Force Kitgum.

Each week leading up to the operation, all the U.S. elements participated in the DCO video teleconference system. The purpose was to provide updates to the status of tasks or coordination necessary for the safe movement and successful operations of the participants. The briefings were well attended at the 560th Headquarters and certainly by the other members of Task Force Kitgum. What became increasingly obvious to all was the inability of the contractor to make satisfactory progress on the living arrangements of the personnel. This was no small feat and included sleeping and operational "fest" tents, bulk water, power grid, showers/latrines, dining facility, motor pool, helipad and a firing range. The skeptics were quick to say that there was no way the camp could be constructed in time for the arrival of the personnel. Each DCO session produced bad news regarding the weather outlook, the camp and road conditions. The base camp project status briefing was coded "red" on a red-amber-green scale at each successive update. Even the optimists were beginning to wonder whether anyone would be able to move any personnel and equipment from the staging airport of Entebbe, the same site made famous by the rescue of 102 hostages by IDF Commandos in 1976.

As the days grew closer to the advance elements arriving in Kitgum, the anxiety over the delays in construction grew. With hundreds of personnel beginning to stage from the U.S., Europe, and the East African countries, and equipment including helicopters, trucks and HMMWVs already moving via air and sea, it appeared as though the entire effort would be derailed by the weather. Indeed it was not just the weather at Kitgum that was a factor, the central region and single road that connected Entebbe to Gulu and onto Kitgum was in some places impassable. Additionally the heavy storms would preclude aerial movement that served as the primary mode of transportation, logistics and contingency support, and casualty evacuation of the Task Force. Despite the best effort of the exercise planners to add in a buffer of 3-4 weeks by scheduling the basecamp construction to finish well in advance of the arriving forces, the contractor was three-weeks behind schedule. It was time for prayer and a miracle to achieve the near impossible feat of making this all come together as the advance elements began arriving into Entebbe, Uganda.

Arrive they did. It seemed as though every aircraft bound for Uganda carried personnel destined for Natural Fire 10. Many of the people would gravitate towards one another while awaiting flights from Europe to Africa after acknowledging the similar characteristics of military membership such as haircuts, fitness, backpacks, and the general way they carry themselves. In addition to the personnel arriving by commercial air, charter flights and military airlift also ferried personnel into Uganda. Soldiers, Sailors, Airman and Marines began exiting a variety of military cargo and commercial aircraft into Entebbe. These first elements, referred to as the "advance party," were scheduled to arrive early and setup to receive the masses flying in as

Fugure 8.1. The tower at Entebbe airfield still bearing the bullet holes from the Isreali hostage rescue operation in 1976. Photo by Author.

part of a complex contracted air plan about a week behind. Despite the plethora of personnel arriving on every flight, the status of the base camp remained "red."

Carrying heavy duffle bags, rucksacks, boxed up equipment including satellite communications, computers, weapons, medical supplies and the faces of a 20 plus hour flight, the tired but motivated advance party troops were ferried by vans and short busses from the main terminal to the military part of the runway. The short trip provided an opportunity to get a feel for the tropical conditions, landscape, and some interesting sights given most arrived from either the U.S. or Europe.

One of the first things noticed on the military portion of the airport were the facilities. The control tower was still riddled with machinegun holes and just off the runway were a host of destroyed MIG aircraft, evidence of the Israeli military action from 1976. Entebbe airport is forever famous in the annals of counter-terrorism thanks to Operation Thunderbolt where IDF carried out a bold hostage rescue operation. IDF elements flew 100 commandos over 2500 miles to conduct a 90-minute rescue operation that liberated 102 of the 105 hostages (three were killed in the fighting). While the IDF's casualties were five wounded and one killed, all of the hijackers, 45 Ugandan Soldiers, and 30 Soviet-built MIG-17s and MIG-21s were destroyed. The arriving personnel for Natural Fire 10 were quick to notice how the Entebbe military air tower and area adjacent to the runway still bore evidence of the 4th of July 1976 action.

Even more curious to the new arrivals was the fleet of United Nations aircraft that employed the military side of the airfield as a regional hub. It was fascinating to view a host of Russian aircraft, including large cargo planes, smaller planes and various helicopters, painted white with "UN" markings. Most of the new arrivals were

Figure 8.2. MIG aircraft destroyed by the Isreali Defense Forces aside the Entebbe military runway. Photo by Sandra Smith.

immediately stricken with the understanding that this was definitely a unique place to do business. Military debris was strewn about off the runway, including the destroyed Soviet-era MIGs, standing as a pseudo memorial and some measure of complacency to not clean it up and move forward as a country. As the troops arrived at a large metal warehouse that served as the exercise higher headquarters, many asked if the basecamp situation had improved. Unfortunately, the weather remained a problem and the base camp project status remained unchanged. Despite the novelty of the history and current use of Entebbe, the group knew there was a mission to conduct and the logistics footprint was far from complete and adequate for the incoming forces.

The advance teams were processed through various stations at the Reception, Staging and Onward Integration (RSOI) site collocated with the USARAF's headquarters in the warehouse. The advance personnel were shuttled to a nearby hotel to wait for the storms to subside and allow vehicular passage north where the basecamp would be located. An uneasy feeling about the upcoming mission was now gripping the advance party personnel as they settled in to see what would happen next.

Then, the weather suddenly cleared. The rain stopped, the clouds opened up, and the sun came out. The weather cleared not only in the Kitgum region but the entire area between Entebbe and Kitgum. The change occurred literally one week before the main body of U.S. forces and coalition troops including over 600 soldiers convoying from Burundi, Kenya, Rwanda and Tanzania, would begin arriving at the forward operating base. All expecting and requiring some semblance of support to be in place. The weather change was sudden, unexpected, and timely for the successful work of the contractor on the forward operating infrastructure. In fact, the timing could not have been more precise.

With the rain moving out, the roads became passable. The advance party personnel began departing the hotel in Entebbe anxiously looking forward to preparing for their unit's arrival. The trek from Entebbe to Kitgum was a long 12-hour drive starting on paved roads and after about four hours moving into a rutted dirt road exposed to washouts and gullies.

The advance team was loaded into a short bus without a UPDF security escort making many of them more than a little nervous about the trek. Shorty after they departed the security of the military airfield, the bus driver made a comment to the passengers about "someone" he needed to meet. The bus began weaving through various streets around Entebbe dodging people, cars and motorcycles into an area that made the group very uncomfortable.

The driver pulled over the bus, got out and met another man who gave him a wad of money. The 560th BFSB team positioned themselves on the bus to respond to any threat as they had learned in their Haganah training. Fortunately the bus driver quickly returned, loaded into the bus and they began the real journey north from En

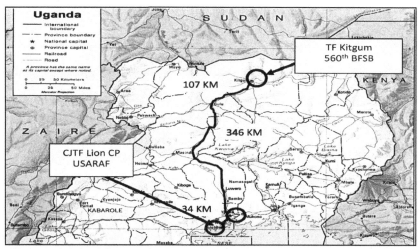

Figure 8.3. Overland distances from Entebbe to Kitgum. The most difficult leg was the 107km from Gulu to Kitgum. Illustration by U.S. Army.

tebbe to Kitgum. Apparently the money was to pay for the bus fuel and not an opportunity to hijack the advance party team.

The trip was essentially two parts, one of which was on a paved surface and the other a dirt road. The paved road provided good progress and offered the passengers a view of the countryside. It was easy to see why Uganda is often referred to as the "Pearl of Africa" with its breathtaking fertile land, mountain ranges and animals. The steady advance ended as they made their way into Gulu, completing the first stage of the journey north.

At Gulu, a maze of dirt roads intersected and marked the end of the easy part of the road trip. The roads were filled with people, motorcycles and bicycles. Already the moisture was quickly evaporating from the roads and red dust rose up every street. As quickly as the vehicles became engulfed in the masses on the roads, they were free of the clutter and surrounded by jungle vegetation again just north of Gulu. Many of the troops found it fascinating that the bus could negotiate the roadway with its many ruts, washouts, mud and a near endless stream of people walking individually and in small groups of two or three making their way to some distant location. Each time the bus passed a group of pedestrians, the locals looked upward in-

Figure 8.4. The road from Gulu to Kitgum was a rough ride for the Advance Party group. Photo by Sandra Smith.

quisitively and quickly back towards wherever they were headed.

After eight hours of near 4-wheel drive type conditions covering only 107 kilometers, the advance teams arrived in Kitgum. The bus made its way through a maze of people finally settling at a building belonging in some way or arranged by the contractor working on the basecamp. The group found themselves a little unsecure about the lack of protection and isolation of the encampment. Nonetheless they settled in for the evening by erecting bug resistant netting around their sleeping areas to stay clear of mosquitos and their high probability of carrying Malaria. Sleep was fitful for the group thanks to the heat, new surroundings, insecurity and loud snoring by a few.

The sun woke the group and each went through a quick regimen of morning hygiene, cleaning up their area and packing their rucksacks. Once completed, they tore into their Meals Read to Eat (MREs) sorting through the various items to find something suitable for a breakfast appetite. In short order they were back on the bus and into the commerce traffic making their way to the basecamp location. After crossing an old bridge outside of the urban area they found themselves traveling on an unimproved road surrounded by tall grass and thick underbrush.

After about 20 minutes of traversing various road obstacles, the bus pulled turned into a narrow dirt road across the street from a school basically protected and supported by the UPDF. The bus stopped at a security checkpoint manned by two Ugandan soldiers carrying assault rifles who looked into the bus at the group of U.S. personnel arriving for the mission. After a brief check, the bus drove forward and parked near a large tree that seemed to mark the center of the basecamp. Exiting the bus it was obvious the camp was in a frenzy of contractor led labor. The break in the rain put the contractor and his personnel in high gear to make an attempt at completing the work. There was tremendous pressure on the contractor to get the tentage erected, the latrines built and the water running before the bulk of the personnel arrived onsite.

While often maligned during the DCO meetings, the contractors were now performing a herculean effort to make the basecamp come together. The first wood-floored tent went up as the troops arrived. This was literally 'just in time' delivery of the essentials. The weather clearing was amazingly precise. The contractor was able to build and complete each required shelter just as that group arrived. As people entered the basecamp tentage went up and as an area was cleared Task Force equipment arrived. It was simply amazing to witness the 'just in time' delivery of structures and services to accommodate the operation. The weather problems leading up to the event literally dissipated away at the perfect time for the operation to commence. It was as though the heavens opened up to allow the troops to do their good works in Kitgum.

The weather factor did not just impact the contractor in the basecamp construction. Kitgum was somewhat isolated in northern Uganda with only the single road, paved to Gulu then dirt/mud with difficult washouts and areas only a four-wheel drive vehicle could negotiate as the main line of communication. This 12-hour drive, on a good day, was also the only route for supplies, personnel transportation and medical evacuation. Mud and flash floods would close the roadway as could security situations. During the initial drive it was noted by an engineer that the road was "just dry enough" for a convoy to move on these roads. The primary plan for connecting Kitgum to the staging base at Entebbe airport was via U.S. Army aviation. The operation required large CH-47 Chinook helicopters to both stage at the forward area refueling point in Kitgum, and fly several sorties a day to and from Entebbe. Needless to say, the weather situation leading up to the event looked to derail both the ground and air logistics operation as well.

With the weather cleared, the Chinooks were operational. A daily weather pattern took shape as the mission progressed. Generally clear skies in northern Uganda while late afternoon storms would develop over the jungle just south of Gulu, the midway point between Kitgum and Entebbe. The timing of these showers in the late afternoon after the daily helicopter runs between the logistics base at Entebbe airport and the Forward Operating Base (FOB) could not have been better. The location of the storms over the jungle and not in our area ensured that operations in Kitgum were unaffected.

Figure 8.5. Rainbow over the Task Force Kitgum basecamp. Photo by Sandra Smith.

Sometimes having a little faith is an important leadership characteristic. No amount of pre-coordination or planning can account for the environment and climate. Long-term weather patterns and forecasts can have some predictive value in your planning activities. However only when you begin the mission can you start to develop a true sense of the weather and its impact on operations. Weather will affect mobility, efficiency and morale and our success could have been significantly and negatively affected by the weather. Instead, the clouds opened and our mission commenced with little impact. How do you explain the sudden and unique weather pattern that enabled our mission to succeed? God's hand of course.

As a leader, you need to have faith in God and faith in your team. Having faith gives you hope and hope provides optimism. Knowing that you cannot control all the variables when deploying

118

to foreign environments is important. You should plan for the worst situation and hope for the best outcome. In Natural Fire 10, we needed good weather to realize our potential and God provided a precise window for our mission to progress — there is not another explanation for the pattern that developed. Having some faith opens up new possibilities when there are none. No amount of planning, effective leadership or wishful thinking could have lifted the weather at the beginning of the mission, keep it at bay for the duration, and of course start again as soon as our mission was complete.

CHAPTER NINE

Breaking Bread

From the very outset of Natural Fire 10 a major goal was to build relationships between the U.S. and our East African allies. As such, we knew that first impressions would be important. As the African military convoys entered the basecamp the UPDF would send a notification to the TOC in order to inform the headquarters of new arrivals. Within a 24-hour period contingents from Burundi, Kenya, Rwanda and Tanzania arrived along a variety of routes into Uganda. As the forces assembled on the basecamp the time was rapidly approaching to set the tone for the operation by establishing the command relationships with the various leadership teams. We needed a forum that would be viewed positively for this delicate set of introductions.

We decided a social event, or icebreaker, would provide an opportunity to set the conditions for meeting the new team forming for the upcoming mission. Subsequently the U.S. Army food service section, drafted from a support battalion in Germany, was tasked to provide some options for hosting our first official leadership event. Our isolated location and hurried timeframe dictated a local effort on our basecamp and not at an off-site establishment in the City of Kitgum. The food service team was challenged by this request because they typically did not feed foreign forces, had not forecasted additional food for a social event, and did not yet have an operational kitchen. With some subtle command emphasis and realization of the importance of our icebreaker event, they were able to produce some fresh fruit, packaged bread, tea and coffee for the meeting. A runner was subsequently dispatched from the TOC to each country's encampment to invite them to our dining facility for an informal welcome event.

About 40 minutes prior to the scheduled kickoff of the social event, the Command Sergeant Major (CSM) and a few other staff members left our TOC to check on the food preparation supposedly going on in the dining facility. The food service facility was a large rectangular white tent with a plywood floor. White plastic tables and chairs were lined up with seating for approximately 150 people at any given timeframe. You entered the tent at one end could look through to the other side where the food service area was positioned. They promptly marched to back of the tent where the food service team had set up our consumables. What they found was a box of apples and oranges, a container of packaged bread, several large metal dispensers full of coffee and water, and a box of package jellies. There was no effort to present the food or even position it for the guests.

Our team knew this was not the way to host a social event, nor create the desired setting. Thus, they immediately went to work unwrapping, unboxing, and generally positioning the food so that it looked appetizing and was easy to access for our guests who would be over in short order. I found myself a little nervous preparing my welcome and opening comments to the leadership teams of the five countries. Ready or not, they were on their way and I knew that we had one opportunity for a good first impression.

Within the next 20 minutes, the groups began arriving. They all wore that somewhat tired look that comes from travelling in a military vehicle over long distances in difficult terrain. I attempted to greet each of the coalition members as they came into the facility and asked them to take a seat while the others arrived. The members of the U.S. team were also in the dining tent and making initial introductions.

Once all were present I asked for everyone's attention and gave a hearty "Habari." I introduced our team and went over the

122

value and importance of the mission and the role our headquarters would provide in supporting it. I articulated my leadership philosophy, standards, expectations and asked each of them to spend some time in fellowship with one another while consuming the food and drinks we prepared for them. Once remarks were complete the food line was open.

The Africans did not waste any time getting to the refreshments, many having just arrived after a long drive from their country's borders. They gathered their selections and politely returned to their tables and began dialoguing amongst each other and with the U.S. personnel. I worked the room moving from table to table, sharing brief introductions and answering questions. After about 30 minutes the place was full of smiles and laughter. The simple act of sharing food together had opened the operation with relationships at the forefront.

As people began to depart I noticed they were not in country specific teams anymore and instead formed into informal groups of new friends and comrades preparing to work together. Each of the commanders took the opportunity to thank me for the food and opportunity to work together. The Kenyan commander told me "well-done, you have established yourself as the 'King of the Jungle' and we are here to serve you in whatever manner you require." Little did he know our relationship would have such a positive impact on the entire organization throughout the operation.

Sharing food is a common behavior with near universal impact among human societies (Enlow, 2003). Anthropologists have been studying the phenomenon for decades and commonly believe that human-life could not have evolved without food transfer within families and between families (Feinman, 1979). Ironically, some of the oldest archeological evidence of *food-sharing* was found in East Africa (Enlow, 2003).

There are two main theoretical frameworks to understand food sharing: *ecological models* and *ideological models*. The ecological models are borne of necessity and are related to scarcity and abundance. They are basically economic theories based on the quantitative aspects of food resources and are often associated with both generosity when food is abundant, to restriction when supplies are scarce (Enlow, 2003). On the other hand, the ideological models look to the value or ideals of food sharing for supporting social cohesiveness. The ideological perspective has been argued as originating from the nurturing aspects of a mother and its role establishing a norm for others in society to emulate (Kaplan & Gurven, 2001). The gains that occur from food sharing norms often produce cooperation and minimize conflict (Enlow, 2003).

Food sharing in the modern world has many connotations. Sharing meals is a common practice to maintain social identity, demonstrate generosity, and often to produce social relationships. Meals are such an important element to human existence and relationships that the two are often intertwined. Family dialogue around mealtime is a cross-cultural experience and often has positive meaning. In many societies, both the courting process and celebration of marriage revolve around sharing meals with one another and family members. Celebrations of personal, social and community achievement often include food sharing as a way to share or reward the behaviors that contributed to success. Sharing food, or *"breaking bread,"* has a long history of bonding people together.

"The breaking of bread" is a common expression associated with both the Jewish and Christian faith. The term was derived from the Jewish tradition of preceding every meal with a blessing. In the Christian faith, breaking bread has been associated with both partaking in the Lord's Supper and often followed by a lesson. In both faiths, Jewish and Christian, the "breaking of bread" conveyed the meaning of fellowship. Most interpret fellowship as the act, or condition of sharing companionship with people of similar interests in a congenial atmosphere. Fellowship finds its origin from the Greek word *"koinonia"* which has come to mean communion, participation,

124

sharing and intimacy (Fellowship, [Def], n.d.). The word has a rich spiritual complexity that includes an implication of action. The action comes from the process of communion, participation, sharing and intimacy resulting in a betterment or transformation of the participants. In essence, you begin "common" and depart in a better state through intersection of goodness that occurs from good people coming together.

The simple act of inviting a person or group to share food is a great method for opening dialogue. The process is steeped in tradition and is widely known for its value in bringing people together. That togetherness provides an opportunity for fellowship and for lives to be transformed. You cannot leave this important aspect of relationship building to chance. While some people will naturally gravitate towards one another, not everyone will feel comfortable eating together. A structured meal event will force people to eat and mingle with one another when they may not have either desired or sensed an opportunity for food sharing on their own.

A final thought regarding "breaking bread." An invitation to a meal is often received as a demonstration of hospitality and thanks by the host. You demonstrate your commitment to relationships by modeling the behavior you expect from others. Hosting a shared meal event places you in a position of influence and gives you the opportunity to set the tone of the event and speak to the group. Thus, a shared meal should be viewed not only from the lens of invited guests but as an opportunity to break communications barriers and begin the process of developing relationships. It should also, from your role as a leader, help to structure dialogue and demonstrate your intent. In multinational, multiagency and multijurisdictional environments a shared meal can save countless meetings, briefings and other information sharing processes. Take the time to organize and host an event early in the group formation process – it will pay dividends very quickly in your group's maturation process.

CHAPTER TEN

Process Ownership

One morning after breakfast but before the 9:00 a.m. update brief scheduled in the TOC, I was making the rounds of several sites to check on personnel and activities. My first stop was the infirmary. This is where sick or injured personnel would report for treatment, particularly in the morning. The building was a cinder-block structure with a red roof. In close proximity was a modern military tent that served as a trauma and surgical center for the Task Force. After a short conversation with the noncommissioned officer and some words of encouragement to a Marine suffering from a stomach ailment, I cut over a grassy berm to the basecamp parade field.

The parade ground was essentially a red-clay parking lot that served as a location for formations, staging area for convoys, and on special occasions transformed into a parade ground or sports field. On the far side of the field I observed a group of medical and dental specialists with their Marine security element loading onto their vehicles to convoy out to one of the mission sites for the day. Crossing from the other direction was a platoon of integrated security forces made up of soldiers from each of the partner nations as well as a handful of Marines. They were an interesting looking bunch walking in a "Ranger file." In the mix were various shades of camouflage uniforms, helmets, soft-hats, different packs and a wide variety of weapons including AKM's G3's, PK Machine guns, M16s, M249 SAWs.

While I observed the group, I noticed several women soldiers in the file moving along and fully equipped. I assumed the women were medical personnel accompanying the security force to provide immediate first aid if required. As I watched the group cross the parade field, I noticed the Kenyan commander approaching my perch on the grassy berm. I walked over to meet him halfway across the parade field. I greeted him with a salute, smile, handshake and "Habari" (Swahili for welcome). He returned the same and we struck up one of many illuminating conversations during the mission.

The Kenyan commander had been doing the same as I, walking around to observe, communicate and support the soldiers preparing for their missions. I commented about the women accompanying the security force and he corrected me regarding their purpose. He noted the women were not medical personnel accompanying the security forces and instead were infantry soldiers. He shared that in Kenya, Rwanda and other African countries they made the step to fully assimilate women into their armed forces. In some cases, such as in Kenya, it was by design to open the military's ranks to women. For Rwanda on the other hand, it was by necessity in part due to the effects of genocide on the male population.

I found it fascinating that while the U.S. continued to grapple with the idea of women fully integrated across all specialties in the military, our African allies were steps ahead of us. We continued the conversation regarding assimilation as we walked to another team assembling on the edge of the parade grounds for a mission. Our discussion transitioned to the integration of the Task Force at all levels including the operational sub-elements performing HCA activities. He was very pleased with the manner by which the Task Force was employing his Kenyan medical, dental and engineer specialists in support of the overall mission. His testimonial confirmed my assumptions regarding the Task Force plan to functionally organize and collectively integrate our personnel at all echelons of command.

Developing a scheme to execute a set of complex humanitarian and security operations requires not only an organizing and integration model but also a execution strategy to make it work. Early in the planning process it became apparent that we needed to develop an effective approach to managing the diverse functions of the force. We had identified several key functions that comprised success for the mission: HCA, security and training, and logistics. Each of the functions had various joint and multinational aspects but were functionally aligned to accomplish a purpose. For instance a primary aspect of humanitarian assistance involved medical and dental treatment. The medical and dental experts included personnel from the U.S. Army Reserve, U.S. Marine Reserve, Air National Guard, as well as representatives from each of the five East African countries. It was not feasible to manage the force along organizational lines but instead devise a management strategy along cross-functional lines for more efficient operations.

Process ownership became the guiding principle to direct the semi-autonomous operations undertaken by the Task Force. As noted previously, the sub-components were organized for functional expertise and complete integration. Each country brought medical and dental professionals, engineers and military security personnel. All participants were arranged into multinational-functional teams for the missions. The medical and dental elements were dispatched to clinics at various locations to practice the site preparation, triage and treatment of the local population. The engineer teams focused on renovating schools and medical facilities while the security teams conducted training and actual force protection of the Task Force's elements.

Process ownership is not a new concept and within a diverse force can create benefits for performance and accountability. Only organizations that fully understand the processes they must execute to support their mission and strategic intent, can effectively move to a process ownership solution. Process ownership supports both functional alignment as well as cross-functional requirements. For instance, in order to successfully complete a medical outreach activity we not only needed the medical personnel but also an appropriate force protection detail to ensure their safety and security. Subsequently, the security forces were prepared, equipped and allocated by the Marines to support the CA team who owned the conduct of the actual medical outreach event. This is an example of an event that could not be organized solely around the functional aspects of Task Force Kitgum: command and control, security, humanitarian assistance, or support. Instead the medical outreach example can be characterized as a cross-functional activity with a defined process owner.

You can normally obtain several benefits associated with cross-functional enterprise solutions including alignment, savings, flexibility, accountability and governance. Each contributes to delivering process quality, efficiency, and control and allows those owning the functions to manage their own enterprise success.

Alignment is an important concept and can oftentimes become a major challenge for diverse forces working together. The organization must understand the strategic intent and allocate all available assets to support key business processes. An example in Kitgum was the grouping of engineering professionals from the various U.S. services and partner nations together for the renovation missions. Each day they would assemble as a team, convoy to specific sites for the day, conduct their mission and return to the basecamp. The alignment of engineering assets ensured that they were all being fully employed to support the effort and not underutilized back at the basecamp. Side benefits from proper alignment include higher morale, greater productivity (as evidenced by the tremendous volume of work completed), and improved customer service.

Savings is another benefit associated with process ownership. You will often have reduced material usage and transaction costs due to the efficiencies associated with increased coordination. By providing the basecamp support to the Army Support Battalion, the processes of feeding, fueling, water purification, contracting and other support functions became centralized for the entire U.S. contingent of the Task Force. Each service, Army, Navy, Air Force and Marines, were not out trying to coordinate their own support requirements but instead worked through the support battalion using their logistics footprint and reach back capability. This can be contrasted with the African countries who each initially attempted to provide their own life support for their personnel. It was only about a week before they began coordinating among each other and assigning ownership for different functions to support one another's camps. For instance, the Kenyans were instrumental in securing food and water to support their neighbors while the Ugandan's were able to distribute fuel.

During any operation, environmental factors and other variables will impact the main business processes. *Flexibility* is an advantage within a process ownership framework. Because you own the resources, your mechanism to distribute the resources and authority to approve redistribution can quickly allow you to respond to either current or projected changes in your process. During Natural Fire 10 the engineer operations experienced periods where a shortage of building materials necessitated a change in project staffing and resource distribution. The process owner, an Army Reserve CA officer, could redistribute his personnel and materials to other projects and not leave them sitting idly by awaiting incoming supplies.

Process ownership gives visibility and responsibility to one individual for an entire end-to-end business process. The single chain of accountability for results and clear role for responsibility and decision-making are often referred to as *accountability* and *governance*. These two separate but connected terms denote the duty and management of the process owner. The external security process for Natural Fire 10 included both training of security forces and actual convoy and site security. By placing the external security process under the control of the U.S. Marine military police force, they were provided the authority and accountability to ensure appropriate staffing, vehicles, training and planning were accomplished to support the overall mission. They had the assets and they owned the process.

Choosing a process ownership framework is one opportunity for success, identifying the actual *process owner* is another. A process

Table 10.1

Characteristics of a Process Owner

Characteristic	Definition
Seniority	Senior-level business experience particularly in the functional area the process is covering.
Understanding	Deep understanding of the organization's mission, vision, values and culture, as well as long term strategy. A broad knowledge of both upstream and downstream activities that effect production or outputs.
Leadership	Strong leadership and interpersonal skills and ability to influence and implement change or engender support outside the process.
Vested interest	A personal or vested interest in the success of the process. Have the ability to do what is best for the process and its customers, not just for the functions internal to the process.

owner assigned within a complex multinational, multiagency or multijurisdictional environment should be an experienced, influential person with either assumed (by virtue of their stature or rank), or actual credibility among the impacted organizations. As shown in Table 9.1, there are four characteristics you should consider when selecting a process owner.

Natural Fire 10 was a great example of business process ownership applied. The unique environment and diverse participants worked well within the cross functional framework. The integration of all the parties at every echelon, coupled with a clear understanding of the support, security and humanitarian functional lanes provided a real world experiment for the exercise of process ownership. The process owners were all experts with seniority and influence. The results of Natural Fire 10 appear to reflect that both the correct management strategy and the right process owners were chosen.

CHAPTER ELEVEN

Peer Influence

As the first East African forces began streaming into the Kit-gum area, their convoys were directed to the base camp in order to link up with the local UPDF forces. As the landowner, the Ugandan commander wanted to account for all personnel who were entering his encampment. Each country went through a brief inprocessing after which an assigned a UPDF escort guided them to a specific site along a dirt road on the Ugandan base. The Burundians, Kenyans, Rwandans, and Tanzanians were positioned in a manner to constitute half of a security perimeter. The other half of the ring was covered by the larger and permanent Ugandan military unit. The U.S. contingent was purposely stationed in the center of the basecamp.

The Burundian, Kenyan, Rwandan and Tanzanian convoys rolled at various intervals and each was led to their respective part of the basecamp. The positions were level and cleared of debris affording the occupants a relatively efficient location for offloading personnel, equipment and setting up for the mission. Each country demonstrated a different approach to establishing and constructing their temporary shelters for sleeping, eating, command and control, and communications. By the end of the first 24 hours all had successfully fashioned their rudimentary operating bases, or at least some semblance of infrastructure necessary for the mission. From an organizational culture perspective, you didn't have to look too closely while walking along the road to observe the artifacts now visibly depicting various levels of military discipline and standards.

After each country constructed their camp, the peer assess

Figure 11.1. Task Force Kitgum basecamp from above. The Kenyan camp was the early winner for camp setup and served as a peer influencer throughout. Photo by Author. Illustration by Renee VanAmburgh

ments began in earnest. The senior noncommissioned officers would walk along the camp road eyeing their comrades' setups with a sense of neighborly inquiry. The Kenyans were the clear winners of any early evaluation of basecamp operations. They quickly put up a se-curity perimeter with concertina wire, established a guard-post, hoist ed up their countrie's flag, constructed tentage and generally estab-lished a home in this new environment. When approaching the Ken-yan camp, you would cross the dirt road and enter through a vehicle width break in a 3-4 foot berm. Along the top of the berm was a roll of concertina wire and on each side of the entry point were armed Kenyans. The guards would check visitors then direct you through a foot path or if in vehicle remove the wire barrier to allow access into their base of operations. The camp was organized with tents neatly constructed, separated and laid out for efficient work processes.

The Kenyans had the nicest yard in the neighborhood and the other countries took notice. Almost immediately their sense of mili-tary professionalism and pride moved them to action. The Ugandans had to put their flag up higher than the Kenyans, then the Rwandans hoisted their colors up. After that, one country started putting nice

134

decorative rocks around the flags and that idea took off across the forces.

Day by day the countries continued to improve their positions and "raised the bar" a little higher at each step. The Africans worked at these little changes as if their national pride was at stake. I marveled at how each country tried to add something or outdo the other in the spirit of cooperative competition. While some may consider the changes in the camps a result of a complex corporate citizenship process, I believed that these organizations much like individuals, were responding to *peer influence*. The phenomenon would serve the coalition well as the mission commenced.

Peer influence at the individual level is well documented in research. It is widely accepted that peers constitute strong influence on the behavior of others in both positive and negative ways. Much of the research has focused on the negative outcomes of *peer pressure* on adolescents but there is also a growing body of literature associated with healthy outcomes (Prinstein & Dodge, 2008). The basis for peer influence is the desire to conform to social norms that are presumed to gain affiliation. The process is often thought of as a transactional process where conforming to specific behaviors leads to identity acceptance.

The most direct mechanism of peer influence, peer pressure, is derived from the power and influence theories and the ability to reward or withhold rewards for desired behaviors. The most prominent form of peer influence is the "*behavior display*" (Brown, Bakken, Ameringer, & Mahon, 2008). Behavior display is a fundamental part of social learning theory and is simply a modeling of desired behavior that is ultimately adopted by others. A less frequently looked at form of peer influence is called "*structuring opportunities.*" This form of peer influence involves the creation of a situation that facilitates a desired behavior without direct influence (Brown et al., 2008). For example if you were to stay at a friend's house and decided to eat a midnight snack, finding a spotless kitchen may compel you to clean up after yourself instead of leaving your dirty dishes out.

Peer pressure, behavior display and structuring opportunity mechanisms demonstrate that peer influence can be *direct, diffused, intentional* or *unintentional* (Brown et al., 2008). Why peer pressure works at the organization level is much in line with the reason it produces action at the individual level – as individuals seek acceptance among social groups, organizations seek *legitimacy* within the industries they belong (Deephouse & Suchman, 2008).

Legitimacy is derived from the Latin word *legitimare* meaning to make lawful (Legitimacy [Def_], n.d.). In the context of corporate peer relationships, legitimacy refers to the perception that the actions of an entity are aligned and conform with laws, established norms, social values and beliefs (Deephouse & Suchman, 2008). The result of legitimacy is credibility within the social context the entity is being observed. Audiences within the context dependent environment perceive a legitimate organization as trustworthy, meaningful and predictable (Suchman, 1995). Subsequently, the loss of legitimacy can threaten the support an organization receives from its peers and constituents.

When organizations come together for the purpose of accomplishing a mission such as in Natural Fire 10, they each want to establish their legitimacy and subsequent credibility within the new social context of the operation. Whether you are in a government setting, military, corporate or NGO, each of the partners brings specific skills and capabilities to the mission. Their sense of professionalism and nationalist pride enters into the social framework that is established and in turn creates overarching organizational-level legitimacy and credibility. From an organization and individual perspective there is a desire to be accepted and valued as a member of the team. This is an important element for leaders to understand and an opportunity to influence the group.

During Natural Fire 10, the countries involved each worked to build their stature in the force. For example, on a security assessment visit to the area surrounding the range, the Task Force intelligence officer came across a Ugandan captain in charge of a company of soldiers guarding the range. The captain was eager to demonstrate his expertise and his soldiers' professionalism and took the intelligence officer for a tour of the security perimeter. The intelligence officer was eager to learn and that moved the conversation and engagement to the next level. At each security position, the Ugandan officer took great pride in introducing his soldiers and explaining the fighting position, its orientation, crossing sectors of fire and the ability of his soldiers to defend the position. The captain was proud of his country, his unit and how they were serving the mission by providing a ring of security. The Ugandan captain was not required nor was it necessary to show off his people and their skills, but his desire to establish his position within the Task Force with the American compelled him to action.

Once legitimacy and credibility are established, oftentimes groups will continue to improve their arrangement within the social context. This is a great opportunity for leaders to enhance performance among team members. In multinational, multiagency, and multijurisdictional environments, the motivations for continuous improvement include:

(1) Serving our organization's long-term interests;
(2) Improving image among peers;
(3) Maintaining or improving our position against competitors;
(4) Meeting stakeholder and customer expectations; and
(5) Sharing valuable resources to solve organizational problems.

A key leader strategy for fostering continuous improvement among the groups is to employ peer influence as a tool for cooperative and conforming behavior. People operating in multinational, multiagency and multijurisdictional environments are representing their organizations and serving an ambassadorial role. There will normally be an effort by these people to establish their personal and organizational legitimacy within the social framework of the mission. This motivation is where peer influence can improve performance. For instance, early on in the operation the Burundians were responsible for transporting the security force to one of the medical sites. They arrived with their GAZ trucks but without fuel. A quick comment by a TOC member in the audience of other coalition officers ensured no repeats of the empty fuel situation. "You cannot be responsible for transportation and show up with your fuel tanks empty – you (Burundi) need to up your game." The Burundians could be counted on for fueled vehicles from that point forward.

As a leader of a diverse or ad hoc operation, you should use all the tools available to you for improving performance. If your role has limited actual authority, then employing behavior display *(diffused)* and structuring opportunity *(intentional)* efforts can often move people to conforming and performing behaviors. As noted earlier, the influence of role modeling behavior is powerful individually and works organizationally as well. People generally take pride in their work and want their contributions recognized within the social context they are involved. When you can set in motion a situation whereby peers are working in a competitive but collaborative environment, then you will see both continuous action and continuous improvement in your force.

CHAPTER TWELVE

Casualty Evacuation (CASEVAC)

The morning of October 14, 2009 was full of anticipation in the TOC. All the partner elements were now in place in Kitgum and we had two days to practice key events and contingencies with our joint and coalition partners prior to the commencement of operations. Today the big rehearsal was our "battle drill" for evacuating potentially injured or wounded personnel. This event was not just an exercise of our Task Force command, control and communications (C3) but also that of the higher echelon's C3 at Entebbe, USARAF, and AFRICOM. The exercise involved testing the validity of our patient flow methodology, evacuation process, transportation assets, communications systems and coordination capability. This would be a big day for our newly formed command to test our ability to complete a complex task involving all of our joint and coalition partners.

We were confident and ready when the rehearsal began. A simulated casualty victim was staged at one of our engineering sites where the process would begin. The radio crackled with an incoming message and it seemed as though the starting gun had gone off at a race. The TOC noncommissioned officer in charge said in loud voice "Attention in the TOC," signifying that something that may require everyone's participation was about to be announced. When all eyes were turned to him and speaking ceased, he continued, "We have an inbound casualty from the Kitgum High School site. The nature of the injury is severe and will likely require casualty evacuation." His cue immediately kicked off a frenzy of communications:

(1) The Task Force Kitgum Trauma center was notified by radio to prepare for an inbound emergency;

(2) The aviation support element went to work communicating and coordinating flight arrangements from Kitgum to Entebbe;

(3) The partner nations were notified;

(4) The U.S. Embassy in Kampala was notified;

(5) The Joint Task Force headquarters in Entebbe began coordinating with the hospital in Kampala to receive the notional patient, and;

(6) The Joint Task Force medical evacuation element began coordinating for evacuation from Uganda to Germany.

In addition to the communications, liaison personnel were dispatched to hospitals and airfields, vehicles were positioned to carry the casualty, and updates of the patient's condition and the timelines for evacuation were continuously passed to all parties. Everyone involved followed the script and battle drills we had developed. People both prepared and executed their parts, while simultaneously watching the episode unfold.

The plan was for the casualty to be extracted from the site of the injury and moved by military vehicle to the basecamp trauma center. From there, the patient would be assessed, stabilized and moved to our landing zone where an awaiting CH-47 Chinook helicopter would be standing by. The helicopter would fly the patient to Entebbe where the person would be offloaded and moved by ambulance to Kampala Hospital ending the physical part of the exercise. Notionally the CASEVAC continued onward to Germany and the U.S. for American personnel. A U.S. casualty would be temporarily treated at Kampala hospital then moved to the hospital's helipad for evacuation. A Ugandan emergency helicopter would move the patient to Kololo airfield where a fixed wing aircraft would be standing by for airlift to a U.S. regional medical facility in Lanstuhl, Germany. If conditions merited, a final movement would take place from Landstuhl to Walter Reed Army Medical Center in Bethesda, MD. The

Figure 12.1. CH47 Chinooks were the lifeline of Task Force Kitgum for logistical requirements, and CASEVAC. Photo by Author.

standards we had set for movement were:

(1) Site of incident to Trauma Center – 15 minutes
(2) Trauma center to Entebbe – 2 hours
(3) Entebbe to Kampala Hospital – 15 minutes
(4) Kampala hospital to Landstuhl – 9 hours
(5) Landstult to Walter Reed Army Medical Center – 10 hours

It was an ambitious undertaking just to practice the CA-SEVAC. The resources in terms of people, assets, fuel and time were significant. However, these expenditures were deemed necessary to fully exercise the system with all of the Kitgum personnel participating, supporting or observing (first or second hand). While the entire situation was a planned training event, the participants were completely in character and invested throughout the process.

It was a exciting to watch the professionalism and experience of the personnel exhibited through the rehearsal. At each point there were small obstacles that required collective problem solving and the entire coalition team were involved and communicating, learning and coordinating along the way. The end result was a successful CA-SEVAC that met all the expected timelines, some lessons learned for adjustment of the battle drill, and shared experience for members of

Task Force Kitgum.

There is an old saying in military circles - "If it's worth doing, it's worth rehearsing." Nowhere is this truer than when you are working with multinational or multiagency partners. Each had learned their own way to respond to emergencies, react to crisis and communicate internally and externally. When you combine groups of people together you have to develop common understanding and procedures to respond to critical events.

During the planning for Natural Fire 10, our leadership team looked at the myriad of contingencies that we could be forced to deal with while deployed. The list was endless and spanned from vehicle accidents to terrorist attacks. From the list, we chose and developed a small set of situations that were both likely to occur and involved life or death emergencies that could effect our coalition force. Each contingency needed a plan, set of procedures, communications and materials for a positive response. We would not have an opportunity to work for an extended period of time with our U.S. and coalition counterparts so our final list of response plans had to be small, easy to understand and employ limited resources.

One of the most important contingency plans, or battle drills, would involve the evacuation of injured personnel. The greatest medical challenge for Task Force Kitgum was not actual disease and vector-borne threats, but instead our ability to provide adequate emergency treatment at the austere basecamp. While we had a mobile trauma center manned by U.S. Army Reserve personnel on site, they could do little more than stabilize severe injuries and prepare for movement to a facility capable of handling complex cases. Our location in Kitgum meant that any potential casualty would endure an over 450 kilometers cross country transportation requirement to Entebbe and further onto Kampala. The weather posed significant uncertainty to travel conditions by road and by helicopter. CASEVAC was determined very early in the planning process as a critical task and one that we would rehearse in short order upon arrival at the basecamp.

Despite some commonalities among the various U.S joint services participating in Natural Fire 10, there were different operating procedures among the Army, Navy Air Force and Marines. One might assume that with a large diverse group of actors in Natural Fire 10 that the greatest challenge to our scripting process for medical evacuation would be with our coalition partners. Ironically, as we executed our CASEVAC rehearsal we found our standard operating procedure, based on an Army model, differed slightly from the Marines. They had trained their process to the extent that deviation from their version seemed "wrong." The Marines quickly adjusted and retrained to accommodate the process variance. However, had we not rehearsed the differences the problem would not have surfaced until a crisis was at hand – not the best time to identify confusion among your workforce.

These joint differences were miniscule as compared to adding five additional countries and three different languages (English, French and Swahili) to the mix. With the diversity of forces involved we developed a CASEVAC procedure from a 560th BFSB battle drill and simplified it for ease of communications and understanding.

If you recall from earlier reading associated with team maturation, the structuring of common tasks and work is helpful in the forming phase of group development. Whether you have a small group or large, training events and rehearsals provide superb opportunities to open communications and develop shared understanding. Training activities will deliver the job and task structuring to provide people with goals, standards, and expectations to guide behavior and judge performance. Our CASEVAC operation at the Task Force level was akin to the first aid training we conducted as a team back at Fort Gillem - just significantly larger. We went from individual tasks training such as applying a tourniquet to organizational-level training for CASEVAC. CASEVAC was a broader level of first aid with similar value to skills and team development but with organizational implications.

Another value of structured training and rehearsals is that your members observe people executing the processes and working within the structure. These observations have a personal impact. It is reassuring to see everyone in the Task Force, commander through the troops responsible for setting up the helicopter Landing Zone (LZ), doing their part. From an employee or team member's perspective a positive outcome can be expressed, as it was by the TOC battle captain: "I'm glad they got this right because it might be me who needs to be evacuated."

One of the most important things for a leader to do is implement the process architecture for securing and supporting the force. Structured training focuses effort and builds common understanding among members and helps in the group maturation process. Standard operating procedures, training and rehearsals not only provide preparation for mission requirements but also assurance to your people that they will be taken care of during their performance of duties. With limited training time the focus should be on the highest payoff items, such as the CASEVAC in our case. Finally, recall the phrase: "If it's worth doing, it's worth rehearsing." There is nothing better for both performance and confidence building than a successful rehearsal prior to an event.

CHAPTER THIRTEEN

The Draw

When working in a multinational environment there is always potential for an international incident, for rifts to develop, personal affronts to occur, toes stepped on and the like. There are numerous strategies for an ambassadorial approach to building a coalition of the willing and attempt to create unity of effort across the force. Of course there will always be some testing of the command and control, relationships, and structure as the time passes (those storming phases of group development). For Natural Fire 10, all of the commanders were hand picked from their respective countries. This was to ensure an appropriate figure was on the ground and capable of representing the country among international allies in a manner that reflected that nation's military profession. Because not all countries are equal, a leader among the leaders emerged from the African participants and the rivalries began.

The Kenyan commander was the emergent leader and an outstanding representative of the East African commanders. The senior officers from Burundi, Rwanda, Tanzania and Uganda all reveled in stirring some competitive energy between the Kenyan Lieutenant Colonel and myself. At first it was just establishing bona fides regarding military skills, special qualifications, deployments and war stories. After that breaking in period the ribbing took a more pragmatic turn and a contest was proposed between the Kenyan commander and me.

Despite proclaiming me as "King of the Jungle," following the introductory social event at our first meeting, the intent now became determining who the true "King of the Jungle" was. It was to be a match of warrior skills. There is always a risk to accepting a challenge if you are serving in the role of the leader. Challenges to the designated authority, even friendly rivalry, can have wider impacts and either add or detract from the organization, empower or subjugate, create synergy or create a rift. If there is a zero-sum-gain perspective, then a win only comes at a loss for someone else. When you have a collaborative competitive environment the influence is boundless so a win does not take something from the loser. In this situation I was unconcerned about the match because it would only serve to improve the camaraderie and positioning of coalition leaders. Additionally, we had a collaborative competitive environment throughout the Task Force and a contest among commanders role modeled the behavior we asked of everyone else.

The competitive choice that emerged was a shooting competition. We would compete using the primary small arms of each nation represented in our Task Force. Marksmanship was one of the training activities used to improve the security force's capabilities and a competition among leaders would likely enhance the enthusiasm of the soldiers working through their regimen of shooting activities. The U.S. Marine contingent was managing a firing range within our area to support the Task Force security training. This range would serve as the proverbial "Field of Honor" where the contest would take place. The rules we agreed upon were:

(1) Three weapons: an AKM (AK-47) variant, a version of the German G3, and a U.S. M16.
(2) Each of the weapons would have one loaded 20 round magazine to shoot with.
(3) Neither of us would have the opportunity to test fire or sight the weapons – it was as though we had picked them up off the battlefield and would engage a target at a distance of 200 meters.
(4) We would fire all ammunition at a single stationary target on our designated lane.

(5) We would begin by standing behind the weapons.
(6) When the time started we would pick up the weapons in any order and fire from any position (prone, kneeling or standing).
(7) All the loading, firing and clearing must be completed within a two minute time period.

With the rules settled and the day of the event scheduled, the posturing and ribbing began in earnest. Who would win and be the true "King of the Jungle?" Among the African commanders there was great anticipation that the Kenyan commander would "dethrone" the American commander in this test of military skills. Of course new information came to light as the days passed leading up to the marksmanship event. For instance, the Kenyan commander at one point had been or was a member of the Kenyan rifle team – no one communicated that piece of information to me until the marksmanship event was agreed upon. But then, I had served as a sniper on a Special Forces team some years back and had confidence that those skills would keep me competitive. I let that information out after-the-fact to keep the rivalry interesting. There was a buzz around the basecamp and although I never observed anything personally, I was told betting was going on behind the scenes. I'm not sure what the "odds" were but expectations were high for both of us to produce a victory.

Crowning day came and the commanders and several senior officers assembled at the TOC. We then walked over to the LZ to meet a helicopter designated to fly us and a few onlookers to the U.S. Marine-run range. There was the feeling of great camaraderie as we loaded aboard one of our Task Force's CH47 Chinook helicopters for the 15-minute flight to the range. We lifted off in a storm of dust and grass and flew over our basecamp. My outlook and perspective regarding this event was all positive and I had no issues with the possible outcomes. If the Kenyan commander won, it would give the African elements a feeling of superiority and that would be empowering. If I won, then my position as the Task Force Commander

Figure 13.1. The commanders having a great time before the shooting competition. The Kenyan Lieutenant Colonel is standing next to me. Photo by Author.

would be secured in action as in word. So off we went.

We arrived at the range and surveyed the site, our weapons and the task at hand. The African leaders laughed and laughed, and laughed some more at the whole situation. They were quite literally having a great time at the Kenyan and my expense. I had a little anxiety but figured I would make a good show of this nonetheless. I knew I could shoot, had extensive experience with each weapon and felt like there was no downside to the challenge. Of course the U.S. contingent on the range was tensed up with their commander being dared to this event – I was their ambassador and they wanted a win.

My Kenyan friend and I shook hands and moved to a designated lane on the range. We each lined up in front of our pile of weapons set out previously by the Marines. It was a clear day, no wind and I looked downrange to verify my target. I checked the weapons and planned to go to the G3 first, AKM second, and finish with the M16. My greatest proficiency was with the M16 and the G3 so I figured I would start and complete the firing with my favorites. The Marines took their safety positions and the range went hot.

I took a deep breath as the Marines gave us a "Ready," followed by "Go, and the two minute time started. I jumped to the G3 first. I picked up the weapon and magazine, laid in a prone shooting position, loaded, and took aim at the target. I pulled the trigger in rapid succession and could not tell if I was hitting the target or not. Without the weapons properly zeroed it was really unknown if any rounds would impact where I was aiming. I finished the G3, rose to a kneeling position and cleared the weapon. I picked up my next rifle and loaded a magazine into the AKM. I charged the AKM, returned to prone position and fired in rapid succession. I finished quickly and again rose to one knee and cleared the AKM. I secured my final magazine and M16 rifle. I loaded my last magazine, went back into a prone position on the ground. This time I took careful aim knowing I had plenty of time to shoot deliberately. Finishing, I cleared the weapon, stood up and brushed myself off. My Kenyan competitor finished about the same time.

The Marine safety personnel shut down the range down so scoring to occur at the targets. Two groups went forward to count the impacts on each of the targets, one group with the Kenyan commander and the other with me. Out of the 60 rounds shot I'm not even going to admit how bad my count was. Okay, it was 19 hits. My target was checked several times by the Marines while simultaneously over on the Kenyan lane the same thing was happening. We met in between our two lanes and the count was reported 19 to 19! Now how do you explain that? Three different weapons, un-sighted, 60 rounds, and we have a tie! It could not be so. We re-verified the count with my group going to the Kenyan's target and his group checking my count score. We came back together and with a puzzled look the Kenyan commander said "A draw?" The entire group of us walked back dumbfounded to the gathering onlookers anxiously awaiting the winning decision.

The African commanders, Marines, and coalition soldiers all asked what the score was. The Kenyan had told me maybe we should shoot again, but I thought there could not be a better ending than a tie. When we announced to the group it was "A draw." One of the

African commanders shouted, "Of course it is a draw – you too are brothers!"

The Kenyan commander and I looked at one another and shook hands like only two brothers can and exclaimed "Yes, we are brothers." We all went back to the helicopter, flew to the basecamp and reported to the very interested and disbelieving soldiers in our command. I was told the information went "viral" across the camp.

Figure 13.2. The Kenyan's presented me a carved wooden lion symbolic of the "King of the Jungle" dialogue that started on our first meeting. Photo by Author.

How do you explain that ending? A contest among coalition partners that ends in a draw. That is the perfect solution. I would have been happy with a win or a loss but either may have resulted in some negative affect to one of us. Instead, we were given the gift (from God, there is no other explanation) of a draw in an environment where parity and camaraderie were already showing their value. The competitive spirit had taken ahold of the basecamp and every time the potential for a negative result surfaced something like the shooting event kept things in a cooperative spirit.

Competition can be a tremendous asset in multinational, multiagency and multijurisdictional environments. The key is to employ competition in a cooperative manner and not a zero-sum-gain perspective. Even the peer pressure described earlier regarding the encampments was a form of cooperative competition. They weren't sabotaging each other's efforts to advance their status only emulating or improving on their work. Competition should enable each player, either individual or organizational, to realize their potential and improve the collective output of the group.

You cannot plan for nor guarantee the outcome of events

during complex multinational operations. What you should strive for is creating an environment of cooperative competition where individual winners and losers still provide an organizational win. The marksmanship contest among Task Force leaders was an excellent event for our coalition building efforts and reflected the camaraderie we were seeking. The result in Kitgum was unbelievable but true. While it would be impossible to replicate that aspect of our Task Force's development, as a leader you can prepare various competitive events, social events, structure work and activities, use pride and peer pressure, and develop and rehearse standard operating procedures to bring your partners together.

SECTION FOUR

Engagement and Operations

CHAPTER FOURTEEN

Dinner Table

For Natural Fire 10, we designed the TOC space knowing that coalition effectiveness is built on relationships and not mechanized efficiency. We built our TOC around functional nodes where participants of various specialties literally sat around a table. Our perspective was much akin to many Christian churches that advocate moving from rows to circles in order to grow not only in biblical knowledge but more importantly to enhance community with others. It was a forced way to get people to look at one another, make it easy to speak across the table and build relationships.

I characterized the functional node design as a *dinner table* approach. Think about it as if you went into a restaurant to eat. You have a choice of seating at a counter/bar (linear) or a table. Which do you think facilitates communications? Of course the table, because it allows you to view each other, observe body language and talk. The dinner table perspective was how we chose to design our TOC, and it worked. In addition to the table layout, our TOC included flex space and plenty of chairs to ensure that all could be included in the "table talk" and not separated due to limitations of furniture.

The allocation and use of space sends subtle but powerful messages in an organization. The study of space related non-verbal behavior is called *Proxemics*. Proxemics research in organizational behavior has identified three types of space important for categorizing: fixed-feature space, semi-fixed-feature space and informal space (Daniels & Spiker, 1991). The fixed-feature space is associated with agreed upon boundaries fixed or imagined. In Natural Fire 10,

Figure 14.1. The open floorplan and "dinner table" approach of the TOC worked to open communications and improve collaboration among the integrated command. Photo by Author.

our basecamp would be considered fixed feature space as would the placement of the TOC and other structures within the facility.

Semi-fixed-feature space refers to the arrangement of objects such as desks, equipment, communications gear, security and other items placed for a purpose. The semi-fixed space often sends particular messages either intentionally or unintentionally subject to individual interpretation. The next ring of space is called informal space. This constitutes the interpersonal space between and among people. According to Daniels and Spiker (1991), within the informal space you generally have the following zones:

(1) Intimate -0 to 18 inches
(2) Personal – 18 inches to 4 feet
(3) Social – 4 to 12 feet
(4) Public – over 12 feet

The physical arrangement of space and other materials can serve as both a symbolic function and channel behavior (Schein, 2004). Initially, the dinner table configuration put many U.S. personnel out of their comfort zone. The area was an open, semi-fixed setting. All the staff elements were accorded a similar workspace, U.S. and coalition, officer and enlisted personnel, to avoid status or other influence perceptions – everyone was on an equal footing. With the close proximity of people and the arrangement in the TOC, people were positioned and seated within the 18 inch to 4-foot personal space. It was not long before the "dinner" tables took on a life of their own and each of the nodes had people communicating and working as a team. In addition to opening up communications among the coalition at each node, the proximity of the nodes to one another put almost all conversations within earshot of each other. You were never more than 5-6 feet away from other work teams. This encouraged and fostered collaboration among the various functions as people would overhear something that either impacted their roles or they may be able to contribute something to the discussion. The kitchen table approach also made the TOC a place where not only could members focus on their own task, but could work together or sit and talk. The opposite was true of linearly oriented TOCs where the emphasis is to receive or present information and depart.

The TOC's open floor plan was a physical representation of the entire operation: open communications, accessible leadership, and a place to build relationships. It is critical that you recognize the symbolic impact of your organization's arrangement of space – it should be aligned with the behavioral objectives you are seeking. Space is an artifact that will make an impression on people who visit and you cannot leave it to chance. It says something about the culture of the organization and when congruent with the stated goals of the leaders, sends a subtle message. With every visitor, we took the opportunity to use the physical layout in the TOC to orient them to our goals of openness, relationship building and communications. We also ensured that every visitor was briefed by a duo of one U.S. and one coalition officer to demonstrate our integration and shared ownership of the mission. Typically, the partner nation presenter went first to keep the African face on the operations.

Despite a necessary requirement to have some controlled access, the TOC was considered a service center for the Task Force.

Figure 14.2. Marines and African soldiers assemble for training under the tree outside the Task Force Tactical Operations Center. Photo by Author.

This directly reflected the leadership philosophy that "A leader's job is to make others successful." This mentality went a long way towards ensuring the coordinating staff did not take a dictatorial approach to the sub units of the organization. Instead, the role of the TOC was to underwrite the success of the subordinate elements of the Task Force. The TOC staff existed to solve problems, remove obstacles, and provide resources and coordination so the element and soldiers could realize their potential within the missions they were assigned. Once again, the open floor plan was representative of the communications and relationships enablers necessary for achieving a supportive instead of a directive environment.

Just outside of the TOC tent was a tremendous tree. It was massive with a five-foot diameter trunk, large branches, and reached about 60 feet in the air. It was the largest tree in the area and provided shade around the entrance of the TOC and seemed to always have several people around it. The big tree served an invaluable function for the headquarters and unit leadership. It was a rally point, a discussion area, a mentoring zone, escape from the TOC, a brainstorming area, and a place to reflect. Its location in close proximity to the TOC made it the perfect place to remove yourself from the ongoing operation and quickly go to where your brain could think freely and explore all possibilities.

The TOC always had something going on, lots of preparation, planning for future operations, monitoring communications, briefings, people reacting to issues, and problem solving. It was somewhat noisy between the discussions, radios crackling, people walking heavily on the wood floors, and the large floor fans circulating the air in the enclosed white tent. The tree on the other hand was this large natural structure that provided shade, color and quiet. The TOC was designed for the short-term tactical requirements of this operation and the tree served as a long-term strategic device for personal development.

In addition, the tree served as both a place for alternate decision-making and a social structure for meeting and informal communications. It was a natural meeting place and often times changed people's perspectives. It afforded everyone an opportunity to get out of the formal area to a different setting in order to change the engagement tone. At several points where the staff was becoming stuck on an issue, several would move to the tree to "kick it around" then return with a consensus. The tree was a place your brain was allowed to think without barriers and explore possibilities. When you said "meet at the tree" everyone knew exactly what you were talking about. The tree complimented the TOC operations completely.

Your design of space should be purposeful and arranged in a manner to encourage, if not force, interpersonal communications. Our TOC was an important part of our strategy to open communications and relationship building. The open floor plan, use of functional nodes, and equal status all conveyed symbolic messages as well as supported the behaviors sought from the Task Force membership. The coordination and collaboration among the staff elements was enhanced by the floor plan. Our TOC also benefited from the informal structure that sat outside the entrance. The great tree provided another structure for enhanced communications and it was used continuously. The TOC configuration demonstrated that even when you have a tent filled with folding chairs and tables, you can still develop a scheme to promote positive behaviors. You need not rely on a window, corner office, elaborate furniture or settings to benefit from a good floor plan. Just ensure you also plan for a place people can escape to for a respite.

CHAPTER FIFTEEN

Primary-Alternate-Contingency-Emergency (PACE)

Early in the planning for Natural Fire 10, the communications design was quickly identified as one of the biggest complications for the force. Our 560th BFSB communications officer quickly went to work developing what would become a superb scheme to connect Task Force Kitgum with our higher headquarters in Entebbe, Uganda, and USARAF in Vicenza, Italy. He would also link our headquarters with all subordinate units and coalition staff. The overarching philosophy was to provide duplicative communications at every echelon. The manifestation of the philosophy was the Primary-Alternate-Contingency-Emergency (PACE) plan.

PACE was an important perspective that we incorporated not only to technical communications but also with each aspect of passing information internally and externally. While seemingly simple, the PACE process was quite complex and included different modes of communication for each echelon or subunit. In our case we had a host of communications equipment and assets available for the mission including: SINGCARS, HF radio systems, S/C TACSAT, Joint Communications Support Element (JCSE), commercial satellite phone service and local cellular telephone service.

The plethora of communications equipment was enabling but also required an expert to integrate and coordinate all the assets together. The Task Force communications officer was the person for the job and he masterfully planned and readied all the systems. Back at Fort Gillem, he and the communications team over-prepared themselves for the mission. They read all the Joint and Army doctrine, Field Manuals, and technical manuals for use and employment of each piece of equipment. They used numerous geographic planning tools to identify areas in Kitgum and Uganda where communications systems would and would not work effectively. For instance, SINGCARS provided limited local communications among Army and Marine units within the area of operation and between teams and sites. However, several sites were not able to communicate to the headquarters due to distance and terrain. HF radios were planned for those contingencies as well as aviation units and African organizations.

The most versatile and reliable communications was our S/C TACSAT systems and we included the net to all sites. Satellite phones were few in number and were employed as backup systems to mobile units and elements. Cellular phones were ubiquitous to the operation and both the communications and intelligence personnel had serious misgivings about their use. The local cellular network was Chinese and although the mission was primarily an unclassified humanitarian mission, the ability to track organizations, listen to conversations and collect intelligence on our mission could yield information regarding our methods and practices. For these reasons the cellular services were relegated to emergency communications within the Task Force and external use was for coordination purposes with local personnel.

In addition to their detailed planning and analysis, they also trained one another to the point of becoming authorities on every piece of communications equipment that was projected to support the Task Force. They would become the subject matter experts on site, and knew they may need to instruct other personnel once in Africa. They also went to great lengths to collect, document, assemble and pack the myriad of systems that would be brought into the theater of operations. Each radio system and associated accessories were catalogued and loaded in black tough boxes with inventory sheets prepared in triplicate. If we needed to find a piece of equipment we could go straight to the inventory sheet taped to the outside of the box to quickly get to the required item. If we were to lose a box during deployment, we could immediately identify our missing items and adjust accordingly. The team was detail oriented, well prepared and part of the advance party. They would need to immediately establish communications once on location in Kitgum.

As mentioned earlier, the PACE plan was a complex set of communications equipment and protocols that were planned and executed by echelon, by net, and for specific lines of communications. For instance, during the planning phase each location that we expected to occupy throughout the operation was identified on a map. All of the medical sites, construction and other locales were plotted in relation to the headquarters. Each location was then looked at though the PACE lens to identify what modes of communication would work. There were some sites we could reach primary using a tactical SINCGARS. Others were outside the range or masked by terrain and their primary means of communications might be HF radios. Still others may be in on the edge of the HF characteristics and the most secure net would be S/C TACSAT. Lastly, we had the commercial satellite phones and Chinese-networked cellular service for emergency purposes.

Keeping all the systems at an operational level required physical, intellectual and actual energy. The communications officer and his team worked tirelessly to assemble the systems. The arrangement entailed unloading boxes, constructing antennas, placing satellite dishes, and moving around generators. Each step involved problem-solving in order to connect and make the systems operational. One thing the communications team needed was an unceasing flow of electricity to keep the networks functioning. The electricity was generated through several diesel generators positioned just outside the TOC. The generators ran continuously and required a scheduled dose of fuel and maintenance for optimum performance.

The Task Force employed a consolidated fuel point under the control of the Army Support battalion. The task for managing the fuel distribution went to a Sergeant Major. It quickly became apparent that the Sergeant Major wanted an efficient fueling program without exception. Whenever the communications personnel went to get diesel for the generators they ran into the Sergeant Major's fuel control plan which included chaining the cans together to the support battalion's operations shelter. Each time the communications personnel went to receive their fuel allocation it seemed they were able to negotiate it from the Sergeant Major just before the generators ran out of diesel and stopped working. The results of the generators failing would have been to lose all the Task Force's primary networks – not a good situation.

The noncommissioned officers voiced their concerns to the communications officer who was forced to address the situation. The Sergeant Major was trying to distribute fuel in a manner that would control and conserve supplies. He did not fully grasp the implications of his management on the overall operation. Had the generating capacity been impaired, it would have brought risk to the whole force.

One morning the fuel situation reached a tipping point for the communications team. The generators were almost empty, the daily commanders update brief between Task Force Kitgum and Entebbe was about 15 minutes away, and of course the diesel fuel cans were chained up and unavailable to the communications team. The communications officer casually called on the Support Battalion Commander, an Army lieutenant colonel, and with great deference to his rank simply informed him that if they did not release the fuel, the lieutenant colonel would have to explain to the Task Force Commander and the JTF Commander in Entebbe why the generators failed. As you can imagine, that ended the fuel control situation and the communications team was allowed unfettered access to diesel as necessary.

The UPDF communications officer found the U.S. setup both interesting and somewhat ridiculous. The Ugandan had been sent to the U.S. at one point for college and later went to China for his master's degree. He spoke of the virtues of the Ugandan equipment with its simplicity and solar panel energy generation. "You Americans have all these satellites and computer systems, all these big reports," he said. "Our requirements are very simple," he continued. "We are here, we go over there, send us beans and bullets. We can do it all over the radio, and hear a snake coming in the grass because we are not running a generator. We are more tactical, we're more efficient." Basically the way he put it, he knew their organizational requirements and he had exactly what he needed

Figure 15.1. Signal officers from each country coordinating PACE for Task Force Kitgum. Photo by Author.

to support those necessities without all of our overhead. They were proud of their system, especially in contrast to the massive setup for our TOC.

The Ugandan communication system certainly did not have all the variables that were required to operate our redundant and far reaching systems. For the Ugandans, there was no running after diesel fuel and coordinating with a person who was so focused on 'his' part of the work that he never realized its impact on the overall mission. On the other hand, the Ugandans were without a backup system other than commercial mobile phones and had very limited access to higher level information. Despite the differences in equipment, both the Ugandan and U.S. communications teams worked well and grew together through the mission. They even performed the first connection between U.S. and Ugandan HF systems - another communications breakthrough for the operation

We exercised PACE both internally and externally across our

communications enterprise. In addition to the sub-units of the Task Force, the headquarters itself exercised a PACE protocol with Entebbe and Vicenza. We used TACSAT, HF radios, commercial satellite phones, local GSM mobile phones and had a Joint Communications Support Element (JSCE) attached to our headquarters. A JCSE is a team of active, Guard and Reserve personnel who can globally deploy within hours of notification to provide communication packages tailored to meet the needs of specific missions or headquarters. The JCSE provided voice over internet protocol (VOIP) phones, access to the commercial internet, access to the DOD network, with an advertised "24/7" capability (JCSE, 2014). Even with the addition of a JCSE we planned for PACE, and of course it was exercised throughout the mission and especially in the early periods when the system routinely experienced instability and dropped connections.

Information sharing in the headquarters and among our coalition partners was another area PACE was employed. When you have a joint and multinational force there is nothing easy about passing even simple messages. Lieutenant General Remeo Dallaire learned this lesson during his tenure as the commander of the United Nations peacekeeping force in Rwanda. During the country's civil war and genocide in 1993-1994, the United Nations internal communications issues, including technology and language, ultimately necessitated face-to-face messaging and runners to communicate to his Belgian, Ghanaian, Tunisian and Bangladeshi forces spread across the country. The communications problems compounded the dysfunctional response effort and hindered the ability of the United Nation's forces to protect themselves and others (Dallaire, 2003).

Recognizing the potential for communications issues ourselves, we would hold daily update meetings at 9:00 a.m. and 5:00 p.m., send messages across our local area network, post messages on a board in the TOC, use the local HF net, and still had to send runners every night into our East African partner camps to ensure the messages were received. The senior Marine gunnery sergeant did

166

the same and would personally go to each of the camps and speak face-to-face and confirm details about the next day's activities. "Okay, tomorrow morning we are going to see you at 7:30. Right? You guys are going to be at this location. Right?" You can never count on information flow in complex environments using only a single type of communications.

Communications to the public also exercised a system of PACE throughout our operations in Kitgum. The public information and PSYOPS personnel would develop print media to distribute, speak directly to individuals and groups of people, employ local radio broadcasts, and use commercial internet sites to share information. Much of the external PACE messaging were instructions for people to prepare or attend our medical and other site activities as well as the Task Force's purpose for being in Uganda. We recognized early that any vacuum of information would be filled with incorrect or misinformation. Therefore, the more information and different modes and outlets, the better for ensuring our message was being promulgated among the local community.

PACE proved to be a superior strategy to exercise enterprise-wide communications. From a technical standpoint, the planning and preparations accounted for all the potential gaps in coverage. From a practical perspective, PACE ensured we used duplicate and redundant lines of communications at every juncture within the Task Force, external to our headquarters, and to the community. There was nothing easy about PACE, the systems required continuous adjustment and monitoring, the generators needed fuel and maintenance, and sending all messages using four modes to ensure they were received by their intended target, was laborious. However, our PACE plans for interpersonal through strategic communications were designed to ensure our ability to push, request and receive information was unimpeded – and it worked. Finally and most importantly, PACE kept us safe by connecting communications to all our moving and distal elements and ensuring if help was needed, we would know and do something about it.

CHAPTER SIXTEEN

The Path

By midway through the mission, Natural Fire 10 seemed to be progressing as planned. Teams departing from the basecamp were now part of the routine and this day was no exception. The convoys for today's various events included a medical and dental element to Pajimo Health clinic, and engineers to both Kitgum High School and Mucwini Primary School. The Marines and much of the East African security forces not being employed to guard specific sites or perform security for the convoys, assembled as groups and moved by foot from the edge of the basecamp to the helicopter LZ. These coalition teams would be flown by CH-47 Chinook helicopters to the range for weapons training. The tactical operations center was busy into its normal regimen of receiving reports, monitoring the communications nets, planning, and problem solving to ensure any shortfalls or gaps did not interrupt the mission or impact the personnel working their tasks.

At about 2:00 p.m., the TOC received a communications on the cellular telephone net from the engineer operation at the Kitgum high school. The PACE communications at the site were active and the cellular net was the emergency medium if the other systems failed to immediately connect to the headquarters. A report came that one of the Task Force's African engineers had sustained a traumatic injury to the head from falling debris and needed immediate movement to the Task Force's triage and medical care center.

The Task Force had spent considerable time early in its formation planning for such an emergency and all the key players immediately followed the standard operating procedure to extract the soldier from the site and prepare for treatment in the trauma center. The TOC noncommissioned officer (First Sergeant) was ready for the event. He received confirmation that the soldier was being returned by vehicle from the high school to the basecamp and would arrive in approximately 15 minutes. He readied the aviation coordination element to prepare a CH47 Chinook for potential medical evacuation to Entebbe if necessary, and directed communications with the higher headquarters to inform them of the injury and possible transportation. The message was transmitted using duplicative means including the S/C TACSAT, through the JCSE network using a chat function, as well as over the satellite phone to ensure the information was received. As soon as those tasks were completed he sprinted over to the trauma center to assist as necessary.

When he arrived at the trauma center the Army Reserve team was fully prepared to receive the injured person. Despite its nondescript external appearance in a military tent, this facility was completely outfitted with modern equipment and had supplies on hand to handle all but the most grave of emergencies. One item of concern was the potential for traumatic brain injury given the report of a blow to the head of the stricken soldier. While the medical team made final adjustments for the incoming casualty, a vehicle rushed up to the center and the soldier, a Ugandan engineer, was offloaded. The First Sergeant moved quickly to the ambulance and saw the injured soldier positioned on a makeshift stretcher with his head blocked between two boots for support. It was clear he had significant facial trauma by the amount of blood. The First Sergeant helped unload the individual from the vehicle and stood by to provide any support that may be required.

The physicians and medical team went to work in a flurry of professionalism that only comes from years of experience. They stabilized the Ugandan soldier and decided it prudent to evacuate to higher levels of treatment given the head injury. That meant exercising the aerial CASEVAC process to Entebbe and onto a hospital in Kampala. The First Sergeant assisted the medical staff by loading the Ugandan soldier, now in a modern military stretcher with appropriate bracing, intravenous fluids and freshly dressed bandages into an ambulance for the ½ mile transport to the helipad.

As the ambulance turned on the grass landing strip, the CH47 Chinook was already prepped and ready to takeoff. Both sets of rotor blades were spinning on the large helicopter and the crew chief was standing to the rear of the aircraft to direct the loading of the injured Ugandan soldier and accompanying medical personnel. The ambulance drove to a safe distance from the rotating blades of the helicopter and parked so that the injured Ugandan could be offloaded and enter through the rear cargo ramp of the helicopter. The First Sergeant and medical team quickly carried the stretcher and medical gear over to the aircraft. They moved as a team onto the aircraft ramp and into a stable position for transportation. While the casualty was being secured in the aircraft the ambulance departed the airfield.

After the injured soldier was safely onboard, the First Sergeant raced out of the rear of the helicopter and crouched in the tall grass a safe distance from the churning rotors. The helicopter took off in a rush of air, dust and ground debris the pelted the First Sergeant who was now the only remaining person on the LZ. The scene went from stressful, chaotic and noisy to almost silent in a few minutes.

For the First Sergeant, the day had already been a long one when the CASEVAC call came in. Now after sprinting to the medical tent, loading and unloading the casualty and the stress of the whole situation subsided, he was physically and emotionally drained. He stood there covered in sweat and dirt blown up form the rotor-wash of the helicopter and thought, "Man, am I smoked." His first desire for relief was to take a short walk to the "cantina" where a local Ugandan sold sodas and snacks on the basecamp. He envisioned buying a cold drink and sitting down for a few moments. His next objective was set – he was heading to the cantina.

The First Sergeant had two options to get to his objective: he could walk along the road or go overland. The road option meant crossing back across the LZ and put him along a well traveled but longer route, or he could take a direct route through the African bush for about a ¼ mile. The road option was double the distance and he was tired so he decided to take the straightest path. The First Sergeant set off cross-country and began weaving his way through the tall grass and underbrush between the helipad and the cantina.

As he was walking though the bush, he came across one of

Figure 16.1. Children travel on a well used path between villages. Photo by Sandra Smith.

the small Bantu huts inhabited by the UPDF soldiers based in Kitgum. One of the soldiers came out of the hut, looked at the First Sergeant and exclaimed in an urgent tone, "Hey mister, hey mister, get over here!" The First Sergeant sensing something was wrong moved out of the grass and to the soldier standing outside his hut. The Ugandan soldier quickly and in an animated fashion exclaimed "Do not walk through the grass, do not walk through the grass!" At that, the First Sergeant noticed that there were paths through the grass that looked like they had been there for a century. They were beaten down and well worn from years of travel. The Ugandan soldier closed the conversation with, "We do not ever get off the path, never!"

It immediately dawned on the First Sergeant, the Ugandan soldier was speaking from the wisdom gleaned from experience and training in the area. There were things in the grass and brush that could kill you – poisonous snakes, hyenas, lions, etc... The Ugandan soldier saw this American who simply thought from his perspective

172

the most direct route was the best and would find it ridiculous that you would need to follow winding paths to get to where you wanted to go. The Ugandan soldier took the time to correct this judgment error and instill in the newcomer what was common knowledge by Ugandans regarding the dangers in their areas – stay out of the grass and underbrush!

This story highlights another important concept leaders must embrace when working with other people, especially in foreign or unfamiliar environments – listen to the people on the ground. There is often a temptation by Americans and other western allies that our collective experiences and education provide us with the best view and methodology to conduct business. This perception is a total fallacy. When building a coalition or integrating different cultures into your organization, you must demonstrate maturity, understanding, and most importantly respect for what others know and bring to the operation.

It is very difficult to teach people the behaviors necessary to build trust among your partners. You can provide cultural presentations, have role playing scenarios, learn language and social skills. However, until you actually come face-to-face with others and interact with them as equals, will you bridge the tendency to view your worth and value greater than theirs. A leader must prepare their team members with educational elements always realizing that the greatest demonstration of respect is through your actions and the steps you take toward your partners. If your demeanor or attitude appears to look down on your allies they will see it, sense it, and your relationships will suffer.

The Marine security forces did a super job demonstrating respect and deference to their coalition partners. For example, they would lead a class on a particular U.S. weapon system or piece of equipment and then yield the floor to an African partner. They would effortlessly move from "leader to learner" in a genuine manner.

For the Navy Seabees, they were awed by the ingenuity and

work ethic of the Africans. The Americans observed in utter amazement how the local Ugandans would dig wells. They first used shovels, then sticks and then used their hands. They would work their hearts out and not just for their family but for their community. After one long day of renovations, I asked a Seabee what he thought of his counterparts and he said with a chuckle "These are the hard-est working people he ever worked with, but UNSAFE!" The Seabees were constantly trying to ensure the workers used safety harnesses, helmets and other protective gear only to find them balancing on a pole carrying a huge piece of glass or other material.

Figure 16.2. The Seabees were impressed with the African work ethic and ingenuity at the work sites. Photo by Tiffany Sneed.

In addition to the Sea-bees acknowledgement of the work ethic, the African's ability to overcome obstacles to the building process also left them in awe of their capabilities. The Africans would quickly assemble apparatuses for moving heavy objectives, making their own bricks on site and leave nothing unused. On the other hand, the Seabees were more comfortable employing heavy equipment, prefabricated material and always having excess. Throughout the operation the lead changed between the locals and the visitors. At some points, the locals guided the way and our people learned. At other junctures we took the lead with the locals in an apprentice role. Respect was earned in both situations.

Listening to the people closest to the action can keep you from venturing through the wrong fields. In the days before a big ceremony to celebrate the opening of the newly renovated Kitgum High School, the Task Force intelligence and force protection team went to the location to ensure that all the security protocols were being followed. They decided to walk the perimeter as part of their site assessment and came across a grassy area near the kids' housing. The team was about midway through the field when all the children came out and started waving. Then the kids started pointing which seemed kind of strange to the intelligence team. Suddenly it dawned on the Americans as they noticed all the clumps of grass upside down – they were trekking through the kids' bathroom. At this point they could continue through the human feces or return they way they came at great personal and professional humility. They acknowledged to the kids they were now 'caught' in the latrine bringing tremendous laughter among their onlookers. The team carefully negotiated their way out with the children laughing, giggling and rolling all over watching the American team in the crap field. Back at the TOC, we all had a great laugh at the story made even more humorous because it was an intelligence team that wandered into the 'dangerous' territory. If they had just asked someone about the site before venturing forward maybe they would not have had to burn their boots. Sometimes listening to those on the ground can literally keep you from stepping in it!

Another example of local wisdom occurred after a visit by our higher headquarters. A group of high-ranking coalition officers came out for a day-trip to see the Task Force operations in action. They arrived by helicopter, were escorted to several of the medical and engineer sites to view the proceedings, and then departed back to Entebbe. The group of very important persons (VIPs) noticed all the people in line awaiting medical attention in the hot sun. The result was a sudden urge by the VIPs to see our team provide water to these people in order to ease their suffering. It seemed like a logical idea although it posed some immediate logistics issues to such a request including where do we get 1,000 water bottles per day, per medical site and how do we distribute them to the population?

As the TOC staff started deliberations on water distribution, we involved those with first-hand knowledge of the community, our ever present and engaging CA and PSYOPS teams. Their input was straightforward and practical: the people should not be provided water bottles while awaiting treatment. Incredulous as this may have sounded, their rational was based on an intimate understanding of the local people and their needs. Water bottles would not have been used for drinking while awaiting medical care. Instead they would be saved for cooking at a later date. Because the bottles would be saved they would also become a target for thievery and potential assaults. We wisely listened, confirmed the assumptions with local community leaders and dispensed with the suggestion.

Leaders should assume they do not have all the facts regarding a situation particularly when operating in unfamiliar areas. You need to defer to others and especially those with first-hand knowledge. This requires you to be engaging, approachable and humble. You have to demonstrate genuine respect for others and what they can contribute. Reference the First Sergeant in this story, he was a veteran Special Forces noncommissioned officer with multiple tours of duty in Central America and Southwest Asia. His training and experience in traversing difficult terrain were unsurpassed. However, he was a novice to Africa and respected the locals for their wisdom. How did he finally get to the cantina? By using those ancient paths of course.

CHAPTER SEVENTEEN

Making it Personal

When an outside entity enters the space of another, even for the general good, it can create friction among local organizations and stress for the population. As such, the process of engendering support from various constituencies and stakeholders is important for the newcomer to become accepted. To shape local perceptions through communications you have to first recognize that for many, the unpredictable and unknown are scary conditions. In northern Uganda and particularly the area surrounding Kitgum, a military presence has not always been equated to freedom and peace by the populace. Subsequently when five countries suddenly arrive and set up camp in the local area, in short order it can throw out the daily routine. Despite the attempts by the UPDF and local government officials to communicate the objectives of Natural Fire 10 prior to its commencement, it was obvious to many of us that there was concern from the outset by a growing number of actors.

Local NGO's were the first to express their personal, and perhaps the entire local community's, misunderstanding of the operation and its desired end state. Kitgum is the host to nearly every internationally recognized NGO and as well as numerous faith-based organizations. These brave and selfless servants all have a role attempting to assist the local inhabitants, as well as displaced persons from Sudan, survive and thrive in the post-conflict period.

To address the perceptions of these important and influential stakeholders a meeting was established to bring together key players from the U.S. Embassy staff, Task Force command, UPDF and local government. The objective was to alleviate their concerns and communicate the good news of the mission and its impact on the local community. Our convoy of two vehicles arrived at a gated compound in plenty of time for the meeting. We parked outside the facility and said hello to group of young children dressed in school uniforms, a reminder of whom we were here to serve. Our group entered through a blue gate and were guided to concrete block structure that would serve as the meeting place. I entered the building to find approximately 60 people crowded into a hot, standing-room only conference chamber. You could sense the tension and it wasn't the heat, there were angry people in the audience.

Figure 17.1. Children smiling at us prior to the NGO meeting. A great reminder of the importance of the collective missions of our Task Force and the NGO's in Kitgum. Photo by Author.

The facilitator began by welcoming all and briefly introducing the main participants. She then passed the conversation to the mayor. He spoke a few words encouraging dialogue among all parties who each contributed to Kitgum's well being and then the questions started. Clearly a "stump-the-chump" attitude was the main approach. While the Embassy team, UPDF, and Task Force Kitgum CA Officer in Charge attempted to answer questions, they were constantly one-upped by the next inquiry. Having some experience with NGO's, I knew coming into this environment that they typically fell within one of three categories:

> (1) They do not want anything to do with the military in order to keep their neutrality in check;
> (2) They are concerned that someone will step into their specific support and upset the work they have done, and/or;
> (3) They are skeptical of what expectations, promises

or other things may be left behind by the military and how they (NGO) will have to respond after the redeployment.

NGOs realize the importance of sustainability, self-sufficiency and self-reliance. I recalled hearing how one of the first interactions between a Task Force dentist and an NGO representative during a coordination visit for an upcoming medical event turned sour. The dentist brought small packs of toothpaste/toothbrushes to give out and the NGO representative was pretty upset. The NGO representative understood that once it's gone, it is gone. If you teach someone to brush their teeth and then there is no way to sustain the activity it becomes another frustrating and demoralizing aspect for the person. Many of the NGOs want to deliver only things that people really need and can sustain.

As the questions continued the body language in the room said it all, arms crossed, angry voices, pointing, etc... It was clear that most arrived charactering all three categories. They were not interested in constructive dialogue and intent of showing their displeasure of the operation by pointing out things that would go wrong or had not been addressed. Despite the calm responses by the coalition team representatives, the meeting was going nowhere. And that's when I received an epiphany.

Over the years I have made an effort to tithe, sometimes successful and sometimes not reaching my goals. Overall I have given a lot of resources to charity organizations. I oftentimes chose to give wide and not deep meaning many charities with some resources instead a few with all. What became clear to me in the room is that I had given money to about 75% of the charities at one time or another. The groups in the room were very much bonded together by their history and longstanding efforts in the region. It was an "us against them" perspective despite that I personally, and I'm sure many in the Task Force were directly or indirectly supporting their work. The symbolism of the uniform was throwing them all off to the point that could not appreciate that we, the Task Force personnel, and they, the faith-based and NGOs, were all in Ktigum to improve the lives of the Acholi people.

I saw an opportunity and jumped into the conversation. I politely asked to say a few words. The group gave deference to my position and I leaned across the table and told them first, I respected what they did. I let them know that I was a personal contributor to many of the charities represented and pointed them out as I spoke. I told them that although I wear a uniform and serve as a Soldier, I am also a human being, a father with two daughters, a husband and someone that cares about our fellow man. I expressed that many of the Task Force were also likely contributors to their organizations. I also let them know the U.S. portion of the Task Force was comprised of primarily Reservist and National Guard personnel. They volunteered to leave their families and jobs in order to support the mission due in part because of the potential to make a difference in lives of other people. Essentially I suggested that like the NGO and other representatives, and despite the military look, we were here out of a sense of purpose and compassion to make things better during our tenure.

By stepping away from the uniform and personalizing the conversation, the tone changed almost immediately. People's arms became uncrossed, they leaned in and a positive dialogue started. One representative from World Vision who had missed my comments in order to take a phone call asked to say a something to the group. He stood up and said "I have been listening to all your questions and concerns and I must say something. Do you really think the people of Kitgum care about your issues? Or, will they be thankful to have an opportunity, possibly the first time in their life, to see a doctor or a dentist." That commentary coming on the heels of my attempt to connect at a personal level, closed the deal. Everything communicated from that point forward was in a constructive and collaborative. "How can we help? Can we have some lessons learned after you leave? Will the Ugandan government ensure increased follow-on care to those who have been seen by the Task Force doctors?"

The international and multicultural aspects of many organizations require the ability to communicate effectively. *Intercultural communications* is a term used to describe the sharing of information across different cultures and groups. During initial interactions there is always a temptation to dismiss the differences and simply try to find common ground.

Figure 17.2. Posing with the World Vision representative following the NGO meeting. When I returned to the U.S., I immediately sponsored another child through thier organization. Photo by Author.

However, ignoring differences often adds to communications problems in the long run (Chiaramonte & Adria, 1994). Instead, understanding the cultural differences and their perspectives will often create opportunities to bridge instead of bypass differences.

There are four aspects of intercultural communication you should consider during interactions with different cultures or groups: *language, perception, rules* and *direction*. The *language* aspect can be very difficult due to the complexity of linguistics. *Linguistics* refers to the study of language form, meaning, and context.

A good example of the language aspect in action occurred at one of the medical team missions. The Task Force medical officer was speaking to the chief headmaster or chief nurse at the clinic. She did not speak much English and the medical officer's Swahili was limited to just a few expressions. The nurse was about to administer an IV bag to a boy about 10 years old who appeared sick, possibly with Malaria. The IV bag was literally a plastic bag like one would get from a grocery store filled with a liquid, taped up, with a straw coming out to attach to the IV line. The medical officer was trying to explain that the bag was dirty and she shouldn't administer the liquid because a host of potentially dangerous microbes from the bag could go directly into the boy and infect him. The medical officer was trying to communicate by saying "That's dirty, yucky." He was not making the connection so he started pointing to the ground and saying, "Bug, bug" to find another way to bridge the language gap. Eventually another person came over and told the nurse in Swahili the bag was dirty and she really should not be administering IV fluids using an old plastic bag.

A person's cultural *perception* is a process of social attributes, thought patterns, and customs. Learning as much as possible about a person's culture and adjusting your patterns of communications may assist your ability to be perceived in a manner that communicates your intentions. The dental teams operating in Natural Fire 10 found many interesting things regarding both the physical qualities of teeth but also the social aspects of teeth. From a physical point of view, the Acholi people had incredibly dense teeth. Their genetic predisposition, diet and how they ate made their teeth much harder than what the dentists were used to pulling in America. Tooth decay was prevalent and many people asked for the most painful to be pulled. At one point a dental team ran out of anesthesia and a woman still wanted the extraction done. Without drugs they took out a molar and the woman never made a sound through the process. The dental teams also learned the Acholi perceived teeth as a source of pride. They believed a rotted tooth is better than no tooth if it is not causing immediate pain. The dentists commented that they would pull out what they could and leave as much as possible. They had to adjust their thought patterns and intentions to accommodate the perceptions of the Acholi people they were treating.

The stated and unstated social proscriptions constitute the *rules* aspect of intercultural communication. You want to be cognizant of the basic flow of conversation. This means learning when

182

to speak about business or what topics, such as family or personal matters, are normally kept out of conversation. One thing to note regarding rules, as familiarity increases so often does the dialogue. For instance, as Natural Fire 10 progressed, many of the Task Force members who initially treaded lightly on religious or other personal matters progressed in their relationships. Deep and meaningful conversations emerged later on topics that one might have otherwise avoided initially.

The final aspect is *direction*. Direction involves understanding the hierarchy of the culture. Some cultures prefer a downward flow of information and others prefer upward engagement (Chiaramonte & Adria, 1994). During Natural Fire 10, specifically at largely attended events, it appeared that every important person was both expected and took the opportunity to give a speech. People patiently waited for everyone to speak (sometimes for hours) illustrating the downward direction of information flow in the area. The concept of direction can both offer opportunities to communicate as well as inhibit transmission of messages, as I found out one evening during the operation.

About midway through the operation, I was invited to a social gathering of key government, business and military leaders at a Hotel Bomah in Kitgum. During the festivities I gave a brief speech that my fellow Task Force members enjoyed immensely, and not for the eloquence of my discourse. You see, in my haste to change after a long day of visiting operational sites, participating in a nightly media event, and the general responsibilities of overseeing a large operation, I had misaligned the buttons on my shirt. As I raised from my seat to offer my presentation my shirt pockets were awkwardly out of alignment. So there I was in front of a large audience, pontificating on the strategic intentions and important contributions of Natural Fire, unknowing my shirt was all out of whack. Almost immediately after the presentation (and polite applause I may add), the Task Force CSM came over with a big grin on his face to let me know of my faux pas. He relayed that after I stood up from the head table, he and the others present noticed my wardrobe issue. They humorously discussed it. "Hey, the boss's shirt is messed up, do you think we should tell him?" The answer of course, "No way, and nobody is listening to all these speeches anyway!" Sometimes the direction aspect of communications can work in our favor in ways you never realized. Such as no one noticing your wardrobe malfunction because you were being tuned out like all the other speakers!

During the NGO meeting all four aspects of intercultural communication were in play. The easiest element to overcome was language thanks to the common use of English in the area and among those in attendance. The perception aspect is where the initial friction surfaced. The symbolism of the uniform was a problem. However, understanding and not dismissing the differences allowed maneuver room in the conversation. The rules aspect was another factor for consideration in the course of the meeting. It was clear that the group needed to express their issues so our team needed to allow them to vent. NGOs must work within the social and political frameworks of a country and therefore are deferent to authority. Therefore, I could take advantage of my stature to control a portion of the conversation. The directional aspect in this situation was not much of a factor with European and U.S. people who followed a similar pattern of downward communication. Additionally there was a hierarchy in the room including the local mayor as well as larger NGOs who set the tone and took the lead in discussion.

The NGO meeting serves as a great example of intercultural communications in action. Probably the most important preparation for the meeting involved understanding and respecting the perceptions of the NGOs and their position in the community. Personalizing the conversation proved to be decisive for building a basis for trust. Preparation, respect and personalizing the conversation are important lessons for bridging cultural and other differences.

CHAPTER EIGHTEEN

Talk Radio

From the onset of operations we understood the value of communicating our intent to the community. The NGO meeting was an example of just one part of a multifaceted dialogue. Fortunately one of the units supporting the operation was an Army PSYOP team and they were perfectly suited for the role. Army PSYOPs is part of the Special Operations Command (SOCOM) and serves to support "winning the hearts and minds" in counterinsurgency and other contingency operations. In some respects, PSYOPs is akin to marketing and advertising for military operations. PSYOPS is commonly connected with information operations (IO) to minimize the negative connotation of assumed manipulative communications efforts. Terminology aside, there is one overriding principle regarding PSYOPs/ IO conducted by the U.S. - we will not lie. Using the guiding rule of truthfulness, teams construct strategic and tactical messages, determine the best way to distribute information, and evaluate both the delivery systems and content for results.

The PSYOPs team orchestrated their efforts with the Task Force Kitgum public affairs (PA) section, another component of IO. The PA section was a multinational element with representation from each of the partner nations. Their job was to support the mission by producing a constant stream of stories and information related to the Task Force's operations. These were distributed back to their home countries as well as to various media outlets. In addition to their role preparing new and human interest stories, they also responded to media inquiries and supported various media-related events. The PSYOPs team worked closely with PA although their role and activities were decidedly different.

The PSYOPS team in Natural Fire 10 was experienced and enthusiastically approached their assignment. The team members were relatively free to execute their IO support to the mission and guarded their autonomy by producing outstanding recommendations. Conducting these sensitive missions often requires IO teams to travel in nondescript vehicles and wear civilian attire in order to build rapport and communicate with the populace. This flexible approach was not without risks but I had a unique perspective of risk and reward based on my experience in Special Forces and intelligence. Essentially if you are in the business of covert operations, intelligence collection, and information distribution, you can only accomplish your mission if you are directly interfacing with the right people. In order to get to that audience, you may have to accept some security risk to meet on their turf so they are comfortable speaking with you. Therefore I enabled the PSYOPS team to have freedom to maneuver so long as they coordinated with the TOC so we could respond, if necessary, while they worked to accomplish their important mission.

During the Natural Fire 10, the PSYOPs team appeared to be everywhere. You would find them on the periphery at all major events speaking with local Acholi people about their understanding of the Natural Fire 10 mission and the people involved. They visited village elders, government officials, NGO representatives and held rustic versions of "focus groups," to gauge message delivery. An important piece of information they quickly identified were the communications channels in the region.

The vast majority of people in Kitgum did not have access to modern media. The limited electrical grid only operated for a few hours a day and never in the evening. There were few phones, and transportation was limited. Information transmission did not emanate from TV, telephone, Internet or traveling vehicles. Instead, the primary means of passing information was person-to-person. This is sometimes referred to as the "tribal network" although the term is actually associated with using drums for long distance communication. The only mass media outlet in the region was AM/FM radio operated by a handful of local independent and government stations. While many did not have lights or even electricity in their homes, battery powered transistor radios were prevalent. During the evenings it was common for family members to gather around the radio to listen to the broadcasts. Armed with this information, the PSYOPs team devised a plan to reach out through radio stations in an effort to deliver key messages about the Natural Fire 10 operation.

Exercising their broad network of contacts and knowledge of the area, the PSYOPs team identified a Christian pastor who had a nightly radio broadcast with a relatively wide audience in the area. The pastor had a small church and was well known having escaped the cruelty of the LRA after significant captivity. He agreed to have a few representatives from the Task Force appear on his live evening broadcast as long as there would be an opportunity to answer questions from the audience. This was the start of an invaluable "talk radio" campaign that greatly added trust and support from the local community by enabling us to provide transparency to our actions.

The first broadcast was scheduled with the pastor for an evening show and the TOC planning team jumped into action. Almost all of our Task Force missions were daylight operations so this added another level of risk to execute. Four Army military policemen were identified as my personal security detail and they were allotted and prepared two vehicles for the mission. The PA section coordinated with the UPDF to have a high-ranking commander present for the interviews as well as produced key information to be released to the public. Finally, the TOC battle captain planned our routes and rally points in case of emergency or ambush.

The evening arrived for the first broadcast and the group departed at approximately 7:00 PM in a convoy of two vehicles. It was hot and extremely dark as the group made their way along a dirt road with a surprising number of locals on the route. It was interesting to see people walking through the pitch-black darkness towards the city. Even with the insurgent threat diminished, many children still made long walks to the safety of Kitgum during the hours of darkness out of fear of being kidnapped. These "night walkers" just a few years prior numbered over 44,000 children who each day would depart their villages to seek refuge in the towns and cities for nightfall.

There were no lights visible as our vehicles entered Kitgum and made their way though a maze of streets filled with people. Only an occasional other vehicle, small wood burning stoves, and an odd flashlight provided any illumination despite the amount of pedestrians moving about.

The convoy continued making its way through the city passing an occasional UPDF military vehicle or checkpoint and making radio communications with the TOC at predetermined points along the route. These checks allowed the TOC staff to track our movements and provide the Task Force's Quick Reaction Force (QRF) a starting point to respond or search for us if an emergency arose. I had been briefed about our routes before we left and was trying to stay attuned to our travel based on the checkpoints. However, without a map in hand and the total lack of illumination, I was a little disoriented and glad the PSYOPs team had done their homework to guide us in.

Our convoy made a short halt to link up with a UPDF PA team ferrying a Ugandan military general chosen to participate in the radio broadcast. They showed up right on time and precisely where we expected them to be. A Ugandan captain emerged from their vehicle and walked into the area in front of our small convoy brightly lit by our headlights. The PSYOPs team leader exited our vehicle and the two had a brief conversation confirming the final arrangements of the radio broadcast as well as the route to the radio station. When they concluded, each returned to their vehicle and we pulled out behind the UPDF jeep and followed it along a pre-designated route.

We drove for approximately 10 minutes along stretches of dirt and partially paved roadways. Finally we turned off the more developed streets, made a few abrupt turns passing some either demolished or never fully constructed buildings and drove up a steep incline on a 4-wheel drive dirt trail. After clearing the crest of the hill, we leveled out into tall grass. The trail continued to a nondescript two-story concrete-block structure with a large antenna on the roof. This spot was one of the highest locations in the city and served as the best location for transmitting FM radio broadcasts. The vehicles stopped and the personnel security detail quickly exited the vehicles and placed themselves in a perimeter around our group. Other than our vehicles there were no other cars or trucks in the area and with the vehicle lights shut off, the darkness was incredible. The only sound was the whine of an overworked electrical generator in proximity of the building.

We approached the rear of the building using flashlights to guide our way along a well worn but rocky trail to the left side. As we made our way to the flank of the structure you could start to distinguish some light emanating from a causeway along the front of the building overlooking the city. The trail started to drop and orient to a set of concrete stairs that led to the front of the building. As we mounted the stairs, a person in civilian clothes motioned us to follow him. Along the causeway you could look out over Kitgum and just make out rooftops in the darkness and get sense of how high up you were.

We were guided into the radio station through a heavy gated door. Our host led us up a set of stairs and into an open foyer. The security detail was quick to walk into each of the surrounding rooms ever vigilantly looking for any evidence of threat. Within a few minutes the pastor entered and warmly greeted each of the party in his radio station. He was very welcoming and had a presence that immediately put all at ease. We discussed the format and flow of the broad cast as previously agreed and coordinated by the PSYOPs and PA

Figure 18.1. Sitting in the broadcast booth prior to our fist radio talk show. Note the other participants visible including UPDF Brigadier General in civilian clothes and an Air Force nurse. Photo by Author.

personnel. The show would start with the pastor providing an intro duction of us, after which the UPDF commander and I would each deliver somewhat of an opening statement including a brief synopsis of our mission and the purpose of Natural Fire 10. The next phase was the most interesting and freewheeling part of the show. This was a question and answer session with the pastor followed by opening the phone lines to the broadcast booth in order to field inquiries from the show's listeners. I had no idea what would actually transpire during that segment but at least I would have the opportunity for a few concluding comments before the broadcast ended.

We all agreed to the format and accompanied the pastor into the broadcast "booth." The broadcast area was essentially a table with a telephone and several microphones placed in front of the seats. The pastor commenced the broadcast and we gave our opening remarks. Despite his easygoing demeanor he asked some pointed and difficult questions regarding the purpose and expected results of the operation. To my surprise the phone lines started lighting up. The questions were great and ranged from, "What were the helicopters doing flying around?" To, "Are we building a new prison to house Al Qeada detainees from Guantanamo Bay?" I could tell immediately this opportunity to communicate with a mass audience was going to be invaluable to the operation. The PSYOPs team had superbly brought this together.

After the broadcast, I thanked the pastor for allowing us to come on his show and the hard questions he asked. I stood out on the causeway and we had a conversation about his church and his

hope for the region. We took a photo together and I gave him my local cell phone number and told him he was free to call me if he had any questions, concerns or wanted to visit our basecamp. After the conversation, we retraced our route back to the Task Force headquarters where we found the battle captain relieved we were now back in the security of the basecamp.

Figure 18.2. A picture with the pastor after our first radio broadcast. Speaking directly to the public on his and other radio stations was invaluable for our engagement efforts. Photo by Author.

Over the next two weeks, we conducted another seven radio broadcasts with the pastor and other radio shows. We followed a similar format but began to vary the participants bringing in helicopter crewman, civil affairs, and medical personnel to provide the callers access to some of the Task Force people and not simply the command team. After each event the PSYOPs team would canvass the area to assess the message and size of the audience. They would find new issues and we would incorporate new or revised themes into the next broadcast. Additionally we added instructions for local residents regarding the schedule of medical and dental clinic service opportunities.

The ability to have direct communications with the public was invaluable for two-way understanding. The questions they asked gave us insight of the local mindset and our ability to address their concerns helped shape expectations and added variables to our decision making. For instance, we found out the Acholi were very easily upset about our helicopter support. In general, they feared helicopters since the UPDF used them extensively to crush insurgent activity in the area. The information about their sensitivities allowed us to restrict our flight patterns over heavily populated areas and direct our helicopters to fly above certain altitudes. We also incorporated specific aircraft related points and even brought helicopter pilots and crew on the air to personalize the aircraft. The crew members were able to speak directly to the listeners regarding the peaceful intent of the helicopters. This included how the cargo aircraft were being used to ferry medical and construction supplies as well as the Task Force's doctors and engineers. The message: our Task Force helicopters were here to support our mission to help the Acholi people around Kitgum. At one point, a helicopter pilot even told a caller that if the locals came out to wave when they flew over, the crew would wave back.

Another interesting exchange during the call-ins surrounded concerns regarding the conduct of military personnel. Specifically, people were worried the soldiers might be leaving women pregnant after their departure! We already had instituted strict guidelines regarding conduct across all elements of the force and now made them public to mitigate the fears. During several broadcasts I made a pledge to the Kitgum Mayor that the only thing the Task Force would leave behind was any excess medications we brought and all the soldiers' money. We intended to donate all remaining supplies after the mission ended and provide an opportunity for the troops to buy some local souvenirs at the bazaar we would later host on the basecamp.

Ironically, we also found our Task Force personnel were tuning into the talk radio shows. Some of the staff would huddle around a radio and listen to the banter and call-ins. I was thankful they did not start calling in with the other listeners but they did provide feedback after each broadcast. At one point, members of staff commented the radio broadcasts were really sending the right message. "We're here to help you. You do not believe it? Test us. We'll be at this location tomorrow so come on. Just turn out." The broadcasts were not only selling the Task Force's intent to the community but to our own team as well.

In Kitgum, talk radio proved to be decisive to communicating the messages we needed to send to the community. The radio shows were a major engagement activity designed to alleviate fears, reassure intent, and build trust among the local residents. These radio broadcasts also unexpectedly filled some internal communications gaps. The messages, themes and updates we attempted to communicate to the community also helped our own Task Force understand some of the strategic goals and importance of the mission to the region. This particular PSYOPS operation was a textbook case of engagement with the community and while not every broadcast went perfectly, the totality of effort produced outstanding results and key insights for operational decision-making.

CHAPTER NINETEEN

Walking the Camps

The home of Task Force Kitgum was a basecamp owned by the UPDF. The area was sparsely populated by large trees and primarily covered with tall grass and underbrush. Underneath it all was red clay dirt that seemed to be in one of two perpetual states: dust or mud. Ugandan soldiers occupied small mud walled and thatch roofed Bantus huts typical for the area. Their housing formed a loose perimeter around the main portion of the basecamp occupied by the U.S. forces involved in Natural Fire 10. A short 400-meter walk away across a red-clay parade field was a long road along which each of the African countries established their own encampments. The African area quickly became know as "the camps."

Walking the camps was a favorite pastime of the Task Force CSM. He recognized the importance of getting out there and building face-to-face relationships with the senior noncommissioned officers from Burundi, Kenya, Rwanda, Tanzania and Uganda as well as soldiers across the Task Force. The first couple of times he ventured to the camps he was met with skepticism by the other countries soldiers who wondered what he was doing in their areas. Undaunted, he would causally get into conversations with whomever he came in contact with and eventually they recognized that he wanted to establish a professional relationship. The CSM wanted to see what they did and how they operated. He showed genuine interest and it promulgated a free exchange of information and opened up all types of conversation.

The CSM would head out to the camps several times a day.

He would make the rounds even after a long hot day where some rest would have been welcomed. His route would often take him through the U.S. camp first to the logistics and food service teams. "Where do you get the food from, explain the process to me?" "How is the hand washing monitoring going." Next onto the medical tent always asking questions to start the conversation. "How many people through sick call today, tell me about that?" "Any medical advice to give out to the troops?" His questions were not staged and he had a genuine interest in the personnel and what they were doing. And, his role as the senior enlisted soldier meant his feedback went straight to the Task Force commander.

After making his way to various spots on the U.S. encampment, the CSM's route flowed over to the African camps. No entourage, and no cameras, only his inquisitive nature and quick wit. The CSM was very adept at identifying the barriers to communication and breaking them down. He recognized the respect accorded to officers and senior noncommissioned officers was a communications filter, the language was a barrier, uniform and rank disparity were issues and they all required a focused effort to respectfully bridge the differences. The CSM was focused on building relationships and he knew being a good listener was a great strategy.

The CSM knew that just getting out among the Task Force was important. He would often say, "Unless you work in the TOC, anything longer than 15 minutes outside a briefing and you are in the wrong place." He would encourage and sometimes direct people in the food service tent to sit with other service members during meals. "Go sit with the Navy personnel and learn something new." He would also advise the TOC staff, "Get out there and not only dedicate yourself to teach the Africans but let them teach you what they know." Because you'll be surprised, they've gone through a lot…"

The CSM also recognized that simple conversations were not as meaningful as more philosophical and personal. He had no problem bringing up issues that some would shy away from to produce

196

great dialogue. For instance, in one group session with a Ugandan, Burundian and Rwandan present, he asked them how they dealt with HIV in the armed forces. HIV and AIDS are considered at epidemic levels in several of the countries and it is a big issue among African armies. On another occasion, he asked about Ugandan values and related the Army's seven core values. The CSM approached each conversation with a "What are you going to teach me" perspective. This approach always worked.

It was not long before the CSM had a full social calendar during the evenings in the camps. He could be found eating goat one night, some rice dish another evening, and something unexplainable the next all in the interest of engagement. He had a particular kinship with the Kenyan Sergeant Major who was a dominating figure. The site of the two of them may have been a tremendous contrast in physical features but not in respect, professionalism and values. It was always interesting to see the two of them walking hand-in-hand (a traditional display of affection in many countries).

The CSM was role modeling what was expected of all the Task Force participants and that was relationship building. He masterfully made himself approachable without ever yielding his supervisory or senior status as the Task Force CSM. Others across the force emulated his behavior promulgating meaningful discussions

Figure 19.1. During the evenings there always seemed to be a well attended party in the Kenyan camp. Photo by Tiffany Sneed.

regarding religion, politics, history, family, and other subjects beyond the operation with their counterparts. In short order, the evenings began to take on a Task Force wide social engagement. You would observe Marines heading to the Kenyan camp where there always seemed to be a festival going on with singing and dancing. A venture to the Tanzanian camp would bring a hearty welcome and offer to share a meal. Each country had their own way of sharing and accommodating guests based on their means.

"*Management by walking around*" is a phrase made famous by its authors and countless others over the years (Peters & Waterman, 1982). The expression refers to a process of random sampling using employee dialogue to facilitate discussions around morale, organizational purpose and productivity in order to improve functioning and quality. In practice management by walking around is simply a management style involving wandering through the organization in an unstructured manner and checking with employees as they conduct their work. Probably the most important aspect of this management style is its focus on "*getting out there*" as mentioned by the CSM.

From a practical standpoint, walking the camps was synonymous with management by walking around. The CSM and others in the Task Force headquarters had to make a concerted effort to get away from the U.S. portion of the basecamp, and even outside of the physical TOC tent, to employ this strategy of engagement. Isolation is a common problem for leaders who get mired in the processes that directly affect them not realizing that their real importance is leading their employees. The higher you are in the hierarchy or your perceived organizational importance, oftentimes the more removed you are from the people that actually produce most of your organizations output.

The simple act of walking the camps and engaging in conversation produced more rapport, relationships and trust than any amount of policy, directives or structured events. Recognizing that you need to make a concerted effort to connect is an important lesson. The further you advance corporately, the more important and more difficult it is to stay grounded and connected to your employees. You cannot wait for people to come to you and instead you must go out to them. "Get out there" and remember if you are spending too much time in your TOC, "You are wrong!"

CHAPTER TWENTY

Baby Cage

The medical and dental operations during Natural Fire 10 were conducted at multiple sites across the Kitgum area. Each location was pre-coordinated with local health officials and positioned at various rural health clinics. The medical/dental teams would set up for three days at a particular site then move onto another location. Each three-day event was executed as if a humanitarian disaster had occurred and a coalition medical team was dispatched to provide a medical response. Thanks to the pre-coordination, each site was expected to provide treatment to several thousand local Ugandans for acute conditions such as arthritis, minor wounds, skin infections, dental and optometry care.

With the potential for modern medical care by U.S. personnel there was motivation by the Acholi people to attend one of the local medical events. Expectations for treatment were high despite the fact that only assessment and remedy for acute conditions were possible at these medical outreach events. Disease and other chronic ailments would be diagnosed but care would be referred to the local health officials and staff. The Ugandans repeatedly assured all of the Task Force leadership that following our operations, they would significantly increase the care provided to the region. This was an issue for the NGO's during the "venting" session described earlier. According to the health directors in the area, Natural Fire 10 was being used as a springboard for a new initiative to care for the Acholi people. Future programs aside, as the people lined up each day for care, the Task Force Kitgum medical and dental teams knew they would be

Figure 20.1. Large crowd awaiting the opportunity for healthcare treatment by the Task Force medical personnel. Everyday brought over a 1,000 people into the medical outreach events. Photo by Sandra Smith.

presented with all types of ailments.

A normal protocol had emerged following the previous medical/dental events. The U.S. Marine security element would assemble the entire contingent, line up the HMMWVs, trucks and busses and give everyone a convoy brief. The summary included safety, security and actions in the event of an attack, vehicle breakdown or accident. It was a somber reminder that we were in an area known for a particularly nasty insurgency between the UPDF and the LRA. Following the convoy brief all personnel would take to the vehicles, a final communications check would take place, and a report would be sent to the TOC informing that the force was moving to their site for the day. Upon arriving at the clinic, the security force would take over from the local Ugandan police or military element that had secured the location overnight. The overnight security was necessary to ensure that no improvised explosive devices, pilfering of supplies or ambush awaited the element as they arrived for their humanitarian mission.

As the vehicles approached the Pajima health clinic, it was obvious to the medical personnel that they would be busy. The dirt road leading to the compound was packed with over 1,000 women, children, and elderly men. Some had obvious ailments while others

200

simply looked frail or malnourished. Many had walked for several days for the chance of getting medical attention. While no one said it out loud, everyone on the medical team was thinking it was going to be another long and hot day at the Pajima medical clinic.

Throughout the morning additional people entered the line awaiting service. One was a 19 year-old pregnant Acholi woman who had walked several miles that morning for the opportunity to be seen by the coalition medical team. The day's temperature continued to rise, and the pace was slow but steady into the triage and treatment elements of the medical event. At about 2:30 p.m., the pregnant Acholi woman was finally next in the line and called forward into the triage area by a Ugandan military officer. The woman quickly announced that she was pregnant and in labor.

The triage team moved her quickly into a temporary treatment room under the supervision of the U.S. medical personnel who went into an immediate action drill to prepare for the birth. The treatment room was in an adjunct concrete block building and served as the maternity clinic. It was a damp undersized room (approximately 6 x9 feet at most) with a small bed. Fortunately the clinic had a local Ugandan midwife and one of the Army Reserve medical officers was an experienced labor and delivery nurse in her fulltime occupation. With clean water, sterilized equipment and an experienced set of support people, this was a much better option than birthing the baby back in the village. The midwife, Army nurse, and another Army medic went to work immediately to prepare for the unplanned birth.

The Army nurse took the opportunity to teach the medic and talked her through the examination process. The medic felt the mother's stomach and through the nurse's tutoring determined the baby was aligned correctly. The midwife used an almost archaic device called a Pinnard Horn to listen to the baby's heartbeat. While the three medical personnel took turns listening to the baby's heartbeat, they also comforted the Acholi woman whose contractions were increasing in frequency and duration. The midwife told the Army nurse that it was Acholi custom that a person who helps birth the child often provides a name for the baby. The nurse hesitated but after some cajoling by the midwife offered "Gracie" for a girl's name and "Cage" for a boy. The American medical personnel marveled at the stoic nature of this Acholi woman who moved through her contractions without anesthesia or other pain medication.

At about 4:00 p.m., the Acholi woman entered her final stage of labor and the pushing started. Again, the U.S. personnel were amazed by the strength of this young Acholi woman who only moaned softly through the process. The final push commenced and a baby boy was born. His wide eyes looked around the room while he was cleaned and swaddled by the nurse. The baby was handed to the mother and a brief conversation ensued in local Acholi with the midwife. The midwife turned to the nurse and asked, what was the name you offered for a boy? The nurse responded with "Cage," which the midwife promptly translated to the new mother. The Acholi woman smiled and spoke to the midwife. The nurse could tell by the response what the midwife translated back to her – she liked and accepted the name. Cage was the newest resident of Kitgum. A short time later, the young mother and new baby left the clinic to walk back to her village. What an amazing day.

With all the missions ongoing in Kitgum, the individual Soldiers, Sailors, Airmen and Marines of the U.S. as well as the military members of Burundi, Kenya, Rwanda, Tanzania and Uganda were doing great works. They were renovating schools and medical facilities, pulling rotted teeth, providing acute care, and even birthing new Kitgum residents. Wherever you looked, people were excelling.

In the security training a Marine Reservist from Kentucky was making her mark. Back in her home state she worked in a factory and attended beauty school. Here in Kitgum the young corporal was training basic fire team movements to a predominately male group of soldiers from six different countries and she was impressive. The medical professionals, psychologists, doctors, and physician assistants from all the countries, were unified around a common theme of taking care of the women, infants, children and men. They effortlessly found a rhythm without being directed in any way. All we had to do to sustain the momentum was keep the supplies flowing.

As a leader in this environment, you have to recognize that it is the people who are making the mission successful and not you alone. Your role is to shape the environment for their success, provide the necessary resources for them to exercise their skills, encourage and champion them, and get out of the way. When you have mid-level and junior leaders on your team you have to let them run their show. They need to feel empowered to do their work.

The term *empowerment* has been routinely associated with both individual and team productivity, along with work effectiveness (B. Kirkman & B. Rosen, 1999). There are generally four dimensions of empowerment when viewing through the lens of individual or team orientation: potency, meaningfulness, autonomy and impact. Each dimension has consequences to both antecedents and outcomes.

The first dimension is termed *potency*. Potency is the belief (self efficacy) that you, or your team can be effective within the environment and with the tasks you are completing. The training you complete with your people before and during an operation helps both their belief they can be effective and the leader's confidence in their ability to succeed. For example, at one point during the mission the U.S. Marine commander began to be concerned with the scope and complexity of the operations her Marines were executing. They were all over the region conducting security at various sites, training with coalition forces, running firing ranges, conducting convoys and a host of other tasks. Her gunnery sergeant simply said, "Ma'am, we got it." And they did. She trusted them and they responded to that trust.

Of course people want not just to be successful but also to know they are performing work that is valuable. The next dimension of empowerment is *meaningfulness*. That is the understanding that what is being conducted is worthwhile (B. Kirkman & B. Rosen, 1999). Meaningfulness can be interpreted at the individual or collective level. Clearly the medical personnel knew treating people was meaningful work and did not need to be constantly reinforced. However, the support teams on the other hand can easily forget how important their work is to other organizational members. For instance, food service people worked tirelessly preparing the morning and evening meals for the Task Force. They often didn't get much recognition from the people they were serving and had to be reminded that often the highlight of a long, hard day for many military people was the evening meal they prepared. It was often be the only time many in the Task Force could sit down, relax and be served by someone else.

Autonomy is the next dimension of empowerment. Autonomy involves the degree of freedom, independence and discretion that a person or team perceives in the accomplishment of their work (B. Kirkman & B. Rosen, 1999). Autonomy is a challenging construct for many leaders, particularly those who prefer controlling the work and processes in a manner where they can predict consequences and results. The problem with control is it often stifles initiative, can inhibit effectiveness and in some cases limits performance potential. On the other hand, autonomy can increase risk for leaders. The PSYOPS team activities were a great example of balancing risk with reward. The team was free to roam and coordinate the Task Force's messaging with the only limits being safety and security. So long as the TOC could track their movements and respond in case of an emergency, they could accomplish their work without interference. Without the ability freely maneuver around the region, have independence and discretion to take initiative, we would not have had the opportunities to communicate through our talk radio campaign.

The final dimension of empowerment is *impact*. When work is significant to an organization and advances organizational objectives, members feel what they are accomplishing is impactful (B.

Kirkman & B. Rosen, 1999). While meaningfulness focuses on the value of tasks, impact focuses on a more holistic value in relation to the organization. For example, a Marine security team member on a convoy sees the meaningfulness of work by understanding the value of route planning, vigilance, communications and weapons handling to the safety and security of the convoy. The same security team member should also understand the impact that safe passage of the medical team to a health clinic means in to the mission success of the Task Force.

Operationalizing the concept of empowerment in an organization requires trust, resources and accountability. Leaders must trust in the abilities of their people in order to free them from controls that inhibit their ability to enhance institutional effectiveness. Trust alone won't accomplish the mission and people cannot fully empowered unless they have the resourced with the tools to be successful. A Navy Seabee can't supervise the reconstruction of school without material just as a PSYOPS team wouldn't be capable of remote coordination without access to a vehicle. Resources should be apportioned accordingly in order to the independence necessary to exercise discretion for accomplishing work. Finally, with trust and resources goes accountability. When you empower a team or specific leaders they must understand they are now fully accountable for their decisions and use of resources to contribute to the organizational mission.

Letting your people go can be a challenge for many leaders. Building an empowered force has some risks but the benefits in organizational effectiveness and productivity are widely recognized. Trust, resources and accountability are key operationalizing requirements for empowerment. A good method to remind oneself about the value of freeing employees and keeping your leadership orientation on target, is recognizing that the real organizational work is accomplished by others. When leaders give up controlling things they really shouldn't be focusing on, their role shifts to encouragement, recognition, reward, and capturing the great success anecdotes produced by the members. The baby Cage story is a perfect illustration of the value of letting your people be free to do what they do best. Natural Fire 10 and Task Force Kitgum simply provided the mechanism for the Nurse to exercise her skills, God delivered an unforeseen opportunity, and she and the team at the Pajima health clinic were part of a miracle.

CHAPTER TWENTY ONE

Epilogue: Crisis at Palabek Kal

The apprehensions regarding the situation at Palebak Kal were visible to everyone in the TOC. Knowing that "first reports are always wrong," I wanted TOC operators to contact the clinic and start receiving situation reports. While that was occurring, the U.S. Marine commander activated her QRF to prepare for a possible mission to reinforce the security at Palabek Kal. Our operations Sergeant Major departed with a Marine noncommissioned officer to notify and update the QRF on the potential mission and situation. It was a tense situation and I directed everyone to stay calm and get more information on what was occurring. I tried to present a calm demeanor knowing that my reaction to good or bad information would be the cue others would take. I decided to step outside the TOC and walk to the shade of 'the' tree for a few moments to demonstrate that this was not a crisis and we had contingencies in place to protect our forces and continue the mission on the ground.

While I was providing direction along the "hope for the best and prepare for the worst" strategy, the TOC First Sergeant decided that he had better check on the QRF who had assembled and moved to an area on the road adjacent to the TOC. The First Sergeant approached a line of four armored HMMWV's with a full contingent of 20 heavily armed Marines readying for action. He had the latest news and intuitively went to communicate with the QRF team. He expected a void of information and went to fill it.

The Marines were prepared but needed the cool presence and matter-of-fact update of information and process by which de

Figure 21.1. The crowds at Palabek Kal as viewed from the water tower. Photo by Tiffany Sneed.

cisions were being made. His composed demeanor, confidence and information were reassuring to the QRF personnel who had assembled only knowing that a crisis was developing and they needed to be ready. While the First Sergeant continued to check the force and answer questions, another TOC leader was watching the situation at Palabek Kal in person.

Overlooking the township was a large water tower that presented a great view of the overall area. The Task Force Logistics officer, in civilian clothes while accompanying the PSYOPs team, had climbed the tower earlier to get a vantage on the operation. Her perspective at this point put her away from the crowd but she began fearing for the safety of the team watching the increasing altercations along with an ever-growing volume of angry voices. Breakouts of pushing, shoving and shouting were beginning to occur all across the sea of people. She began to wonder whether they would be able to get out of the area safely if this crowd situation continued to destabilize. While she viewed the conditions from her perspective, a few of the PYSOP team were actually on the periphery of the crowd and at some points, right in the middle of the action.

Inside the perimeter, the U.S. Marine security detachment was on high alert. Each Marine was ready and looking intently for any potential breach of the inner circle. They all had sectors to control and were fully prepared to protect their area if necessary. Much of their view was at ground level and the massive crowd continued to get more unruly and put pressure against the fence line. Again pushing, shoving and fisticuffs seemed to be happening at different locations simultaneously. They were in constant communications with the TOC via TACSAT radio providing updates on the situation and requesting support.

Back at the TOC, conflicting information began to arrive from the Marines in the perimeter, the PSYOPs team in the crowd and the Ugandan military forces on the outer perimeter. Each element was communicating on a different net making our PACE system work and yield its full benefits. The Marines were speaking on the TACSAT net, the PSYOPs team were on cell-phones, a CA officer was on a satellite phone and the UPDF were communicating on a HF tactical network established just days before. The messages were clear but varied widely in their assessment of the situation. For the Marines, it appeared the security situation was completely falling apart and they were asking for immediate reinforcement. The PSYOPs and CA personnel were reporting that the situation was unruly but not out of control, and the Ugandan military responded that nothing was going on that needed attention.

The varied reports provided a balance to the message and our subsequent response. I engaged my Ugandan deputy commander who was in command of the local UPDF forces and asked him to have the law enforcement element reinforced. We needed to keep an "African face" on this operation especially in any response to crowds. The last thing our mission needed was a heavily armed U.S. Marine security contingent arriving unless as a last resort. While the UPDF commander was making calls to the local police, I walked outside the TOC and contacted our higher headquarters via cell-phone to elaborate on what had been reported on our satellite systems.

After my initial comments and plan for a proposed response, I began fielding the questions and good ideas of the USARAF team in Entebbe. I assured them that we had everything under control, were using the local response forces first but were prepared to send our QRF if all else failed. One of the suggestions was to task one of helicopters to fly over the area in order to get a "bird's eye view" of the clinic and surrounding crowds. Thanks to the various radio broadcasts I was a part of in the previous week, I had learned first hand of the fear and sensitivity the locals had regarding helicopters. The local Acholi were frightened of helicopters due to their use by the UPDF fighting LRA insurgents. I negated the flying suggestion and told them we would not lift any

Figure 21.2. Crowds getting more challenging from the perspective of the PSYOPS team. Had we lifted a helicopter and overflown the area the result would have likely created panic. Photo by Tiffany Sneed.

helicopters to the scene for it would likely cause chaos and make the situation worse. The value of directly communicating with the public through our nightly radio broadcasts and other outreach was already shaping my decisions for the better.

As I went back into the TOC, the crowd conditions were worsening according to the reports. However, each element provided a different degree of deterioration. Following the call from the Ugandan military commander, the local police sent a contingent to the scene for crowd control. The police were immediately overwhelmed in part because they were simply outnumbered. They did not have the ability to break up the altercations that were occurring or intervene in any meaningful way to calm or control the crowd.

Another call for support came across the net from the Marines at the clinic. I consulted with the Ugandan commander and he agreed to send a platoon of his troops to assist and help regain control of the situation. The UPDF platoon arrived shortly thereafter and were also overwhelmed by the size and angry tone of the crowd. Amazingly, the medical team in the clinic's security perimeter was undeterred by the threatening environment outside and the medical triage and services continued unabated. People were continuously moving into and out of the clinic area to receive treatment.

At the TOC, the reports from Palabek Kal were still widely diverse in their assessments but they all seemed to be in consensus on one thing – the situation had not stabilized or grown better. That moved me to direct the Ugandan military commander to get control of the crowds and guarantee the protection of the Task Force personnel at the clinic. Additionally, it had to be accomplished in a manner that did not discredit our mission. He departed in person with additional UPDF forces while the Marine QRF stood by anxiously awaiting the order to reinforce or relieve the security force at Palabek Kal.

Within 40 minutes we began getting reports from our forces on the ground that the UPDF commander's arrival seemed to calm things down. The Ugandan military force quickly fanned out across the crowd and the fighting and altercations stopped with very little intervention. The Ugandan commander's personal reputation in the area and the strength of force he brought with him was enough to cease not only the unruliness of the crowd but even the prospect for violence. In short order, all reports from Palabek Kal were congruent and reporting a normal situation. The threat to the operation had been mitigated.

The remainder of the day, the medical operation continued to maximum capacity and the UPDF response force gradually withdrew leaving the crowd control to the platoon of local police on site. The medical team processed over 800 people through the clinic and returned safely. Additionally they were fully committed and ready for a return trip to the clinic the next day. The Task Force had been tested and became stronger and better prepared from it. We made some changes to our standing operating procedures to include additional Ugandan military personnel for the start of each new outreach effort.

The Palebak Kal story is a perfect illustration of the lessons captured in this book. The plans we made to respond to contingencies, rehearsals conducted, relationship building events, organizing strategies, communications processes and procedures, outreach to the community and leadership philosophy all contributed to a successful ending at Palabek Kal. If we had reacted to only one report instead of seeking multiple viewpoints, rushed our QRF to the scene and lifted our helicopters for observation, the situation would have likely developed into an international incident. Instead, by sticking to our plans, relying on our coalition partners and using our relationships to solve coalition problems, we found a balance that allowed the mission to continue and kept our African partners in the forefront. Palabek Kal never became a crisis because we exercised emergency protocols solidified formally and informally in the previous days. In essence, we exercised the leadership necessary to make the Task Force successful. Without that purposeful effort up front, Palabek Kal may have become a crisis and strategic failure for the coalition.

SECTION FIVE

Mission Complete

CHAPTER TWENTY TWO

Getting Better

Throughout Natural Fire 10 there was an evening brief in the TOC attended by representatives of all the elements in the Task Force. The TOC would fill with tired and sometimes filthy participants after a long day working on the various missions around Kitgum. The purposes of these meetings were twofold: (1) to identify current dysfunction or deficiencies in the operation, and (2) to prepare for the next 24-48 hours. Any frustrations were aired in public and the discourse was designed to solve problems and improve activities each day. It was a forum of continuous improvement designed to evolve our operations as we learned new ways of optimizing our business.

Each day brought new opportunities to learn and grow as a team. The process of internal integration often resulted in new partnerships among the coalition as strengths and weaknesses were identified and capabilities shared to improve collective performance. As the coalition team worked together and met each of our training objectives, conducted medical and dental outreach events, and improved facilities we were achieving the end-state I envisioned before the mission began:

> Task Force Kitgum, successfully conducted multinational training and HCA in the Kitgum AO. All participants have an increased understanding of each other's capabilities and strengths, and the importance of transparency, rule of law, and strengthening democratic institutions. All FTX participants completed 100%

of individual tasks to standard. Specified medical and educational facilities have been improved. Regional medical personnel have increased ability and over 10,000 local citizens have been provided medical and dental care. Strategic and tactical communications nets were fully operational throughout the duration of the exercise. Task Force Kitgum elements received all necessary resources/support to complete mission requirements. All participants redeployed safely, and interoperability among partner nations has been enhanced.

As the final field elements completed their last day of medical, engineering, security and training tasks, the TOC staff were preparing for a final review of the Task Force's activities. This review was required to capture lessons and recommendations to improve future Natural Fire events or similar contingency missions. The date was set for a forum discussion and directions and scope of input were provided to allow each U.S. element as well as each coalition partner country to prepare comments. This dialogue would be an official AAR that would inform a final written product designed as a guide for like operations in the future. These proceedings prove useful primarily to the participants involved. As noted earlier in the readings, despite the effort put forth documenting missions such as Natural Fire 10, rarely do those documents see light during future events. Nonetheless, the AAR would be conducted and written to standard.

On the afternoon of the AAR forum not all the Task Force elements participated at an equal level. As the meeting commenced we went over the macro objectives of the mission and came to the consensus we had achieved all of our goals. We moved onto our internal modeling and had a spirited discussion regarding our TOC processes and use of personnel. During the Natural Fire 10, the TOC worked superbly coordinating assets, prioritizing Task Force activities, and tracking personnel and resources. However, the multinational staff was working on a current operations model, meaning they were simply looking ahead to short-term pre-planned operations. Once a good battle rhythm was achieved, the TOC staff found periods of time where the daily events seemed routine and they could have used something else to work on. Our collective recommendation was to develop some additional scenario-based actions to require more operational planning by the TOC staff. This would increase the staff's requirements from a current operations model of coordination, prioritizing, and tracking, onto future operations such as longer term planning and orders production – a more challenging endeavor.

Another area of consensus emerged during our discourse regarding early internal engagement among the partner nations prior to the commencement of operations. Essentially everyone agreed that we would have benefited by a period of additional preparation among the coalition before formal operations began. Our recommendation was to schedule extra time specifically for early team-building, training, and rehearsals. This additional period would also provide an opportunity for greater understanding of partner-nation capabilities. One struggle we had early in Natural Fire 10, was opening the partner nations to sharing their resources, particularly transportation assets. As we learned about their equipment and what was brought, it became clear we needed to pool assets for the good of the Task Force. Unfortunately, that was identified after about a week into the mission. An earlier discussion could have correctly integrated all resources into the operation for greater efficiency. In essence, we learned and adjusted as the mission unfolded instead of having partner nation capabilities and resource expertise from the start.

Externally, the group's early engagement recommendations were in the form of communications to the local community and early integration of diplomatic protocols. As we found from our radio interviews, there was not a collective understanding of our peaceful intent upon arrival in Kitgum. That may have impacted initial acceptance by some of the Acholi people. From a diplomatic perspective, we found a gap in dealing with customs, border relations, and other factors during the movement of personnel and equipment. The gap did not preclude any of the Task Force units from entering Uganda but anything that adds to the stress of deployment is not helpful. The diplomatic element also came into play with our interface with NGO and faith-based groups operating around Kitgum. The U.S. Embassy was very responsive and quickly dispatched representatives throughout Natural Fire 10 to address any issues that surfaced or appeared possible. However, they were often reacting to issues that surfaced instead of having proactively identified and mitigated the problems beforehand. Our AAR group recommended that the diplomatic outreach program begin much earlier to alleviate potential flashpoints that could affect the mission.

The AAR conversations were a great reminder that while we continuously evolved and adjusted our efforts to improve during Natural Fire 10, we could be better the next time. It was interesting that our partner nations observed the same dysfunction and inconveniences that the U.S. joint force personnel saw, as well as many we did not. Reflecting back through the mission and our internal and external adjustments, our use of peer influence, role modeling and cooperative competition all served to foster a continuous improvement perspective among participants throughout the operation.

There is an old Army saying when operating in a field environment that "You must always try to improve your foxhole." This is a fundamental truth of all infantrymen who at every extended stop, must dig a shallow trench to protect them from direct fire (rifle or machinegun) or indirect fire (artillery, bombs and rockets). The longer you stay in that location, the more effort you should make to enhance in your fighting position. You begin by clearing away brush so you can observe better, and use it to better conceal your position. Next you may dig the hole deeper and add sandbags. Then you find some logs and put them over your head with additional sandbags on top. You move from a shallow trench to a protective bunker making good use of your time and resources. The process of fortifying your fighting position never ends until you move to another location at which point you begin the cycle all over again.

The military applies the same "Improve your fighting position" philosophy to the conduct of operations. Improvement is even referenced in the Army's definition of leadership:

> "Leadership is influencing people by providing purpose, direction and motivation while operating to accomplish the mission and *improving* the organization" (Army Doctrine & Training Publication, 6-22, 2012).

If you recall from reading Section 1, transformational leadership is often associated with continuous improvement and change. My personal improvement philosophy is best characterized by a motto I am infamous for promulgating among units I have had the great honor to be associated: "If you are not getting better, then you must be getting worse." Ironically I learned the catchphrase while serving in Vicenza, Italy, in the U.S. Southern European Task Force (who later reorganized as USARAF). The simple phrase provides an impetus for continuous improvement and most importantly the action necessary for better outcomes to become reality. Of the many things I have learned about operations and planning, one lesson in particular is most relevant to this discussion. As soon as you think you understand, feel comfortable and perceive you are in control of what you are doing, that is when change will occur and disrupt your program. To make it simple: "As soon as you think you 'got-it' – you're done."

When complacency and comfort set in with all the actions occurring, that is precisely when you will realize you are not in control of the situation. Your best planner will be transferred, your top person will get sick, the weather will hit, or some other set of variables will suddenly change. When that occurs the system you felt so comfortable with will collapse leaving you and the organization to suddenly be reacting to everything instead of influencing and shaping the environment for success.

Continuous improvement keeps you evolving and searching for opportunities to enhance your position instead of falling for the ease and comfort that breeds complacency. It also provides an environment that not only continuously strives for greater performance but also attracts high performers. As a leader, your improvement focus should not be solely at a collective level in your organization. Processes and systems are important to effective functioning but you cannot forget those components of work are run by people. At the individual and team level is where you will find ingenuity and innovation – that is where continuous improvement should reside as an underlying assumption, or operating truth, among your personnel. Your role, referencing my favorite approach to leadership, as a transformational leader is to instill a sense of purpose, direction and belief that a new way is possible and seek to implement changes that will improve the organization through its membership.

CHAPTER TWENTY THREE

Closing Time

At the conclusion of the Natural Fire 10 operation, the Task Force headquarters was dissolved and units began to individually recover and prepare for their return. Normally during an operation such as this one, people or teams arrive as individual entities, are assimilated into the group or in our case the Task Force, perform their role during the mission, then resume back into their original formations for the return home. In theory, that process works well if you have a specific entity on the ground charged with ensuring that all the units are taken care of in transition and methodically redeployed in a synchronized fashion. Whenever disruptions begin to occur you can expect issues to arise and that is exactly what transpired at the end of the operation in Uganda.

With the mission completed in Kitgum, the Task Force elements returned to their original configurations and were scheduled for return by aircraft and ground transportation. The African partner nations were the first to depart by ground. Their convoys left at various times over a 24-hour period. Groups of 10-20 military vehicles made their way over the dusty roads for long treks back to Burundi, Kenya, Rwanda and Tanzania. The majority of U.S. personnel would move by helicopter or bus to the Entebbe military airport and await final air transportation back to their home bases. A U.S. Marine shore party had their own agenda transporting the HMMWVs and other pieces of equipment to a port in Kenya for sealift back to the U.S.

There were two official functions that signaled the end of our Task Force Kitgum command role in Natural Fire 10: (1) the final awards ceremony, and (2) completion of the AAR. The AAR process served as not only a forum to discuss ways of bettering the next operation but also a setting for *adjournment* (from the stages of group development) among the key leaders who had grown together as a team through the operation. Subsequently we planned for and followed the AAR with a plaque presentation to each of the leaders of our partner nations on behalf of the 560th BFSB. In addition to the leader-to-leader exchange, we had prepared for each staff member from our unit to have an individual plaque to give to their counterpart as well. I had been adamant about purchasing and bringing a whole box of awards prior to our departure from the U.S. for precisely the effects we witnessed during the presentations. It was clear by both their surprise and gratitude that these small gifts on our part had great significance to our partner nation counterparts. Despite being at the end of the mission, we continued to model our leadership philosophy and ensuring the intent of building relationships was never lost, not even at the end.

In addition to our coalition partners, we planned another adjournment process among our U.S. joint partners in the form of an award ceremony. We decided early in the planning back at Fort Gillem, GA, that the opportunity to best recognize and reinforce positive behavior was as close as possible to when the behavior was exhibited. Unfortunately in the military and other government agencies, oftentimes one may do something worthwhile today, and a year later you might finally receive the recognition. The bureaucracy, timing, and a host of other variables intercede in a manner that ultimately seems to remove much of value of the recognition and the ability to reinforce to others what behaviors warrant reward.

Recognizing the bureaucratic nightmare of trying to facilitate awards to units from the Army, Navy, Air Force and Marines scattered across the U.S. and Europe after the mission ended, we opted to go with the immediate approach. This would ensure that our joint members would receive the recognition they earned and deserved prior to departing Kitgum. Thus we brought a full array of Army Commendation Medals, Army Achievement Medals, Certificates of Appreciation, unit coins (given for excellence by the commander and CSM) and plaques for the units.

In Kitgum we started the award processing early and completed all the administration onsite so the awards and their documentation would go home with the recipient. We scheduled a final award ceremony and gave it all out. The top Army, Navy, Air Force and Marine members who were recognized by their supervisors and peers stood proudly receiving various awards for their part in Natural Fire 10. These top performers received the recognition they deserved in front of the audience that understood how they contributed to our overall success. It was a great afternoon.

Figure 23.1. The Task Force Kitgum CSM presents a coin to the medic who assisted in delivering baby Cage. Awards and recognition are best given as close to the event as possible. Photo by U.S. Army.

Shortly after the award ceremony we began the process of retrieving and accounting for all our equipment, especially the communications items that had been issued out across the Task Force to accomplish our PACE plan. We packed up our TOC setup including maps, administrative materials, logbooks, orders and everything else we brought with us. Someone in the Task Force organized a last minute donation drive during the final 24 hours at Kitgum. Collections for food and clothing were taken up to give to the local NGO and faith-based organizations. Truckloads of donated materials including food, clothing and shoes left the basecamp to be distributed to the community. Additionally, with the medical operations over and only hours from moving to our staging area in Entebbe, all the medical supplies remaining, held in reserve for emergency purposes by medics, doctors, nurses and dental personnel, along with individual first aid and supplies were collected or donated to support the residents. These were turned over en masse to a very grateful local health director. Through the very end of Natural Fire 10, the commitment of our U.S. and joint personnel to the mission and the local inhabitants was unmistakable.

Figure 23.2. Packed into a CH47 for our return flight to Entebbe. It was a bittersweet ride. Photo by Author.

After loading our organizational equipment and radios back into the black tough boxes, we packed individual kits into our rucksacks and staged the material in the now empty TOC. The transportation schedule was posted and our 560th BFSB element would be among the early groups to move to Entebbe to stage for our contract flight home to America. As the time neared for our CH-47 flight south, we moved all our equipment to the landing zone where a flight of two CH-47's stood by to receive our team and another element heading one step closer to home.

We packed the gear in the center compartment of the helicopter and strapped it down leaving just enough space for the personnel to sit in the cargo strap seats along the edge of the aircraft. The morale was high and the mood was great. We were satisfied with our handling of the mission, relieved that it was over, and looking forward to redeploying back home and sharing this great adventure with our families. As the aircraft engines started up, each person put in their earplugs and awaited takeoff. You could feel the aircraft gradually lift from the ground then fully power into the air. The pilots took a gradual right and we made a final pass over the basecamp. The team was intently looking out over our former home through the portal windows and out of the rear of the aircraft's fuselage. It was a bittersweet moment.

We continued climbing and flew over the city of Kitgum and south towards Entebbe. Before we reached 1,000 feet in altitude we observed locals outside watching us fly over their homes and land, an interesting contrast from when we arrived. Early in the mission I distinctly remember seeing people literally run and hide from our helicopters and now they just came out and watched us fly off without fear. Something changed.

As we traced south the sky was overcast with low clouds that whisked in circular fashion behind the aircraft. The second CH-47 was just off center to our rear flying in an echelon right formation.

It was a great trip to reflect and relax. The flight took us over the high plains and slow moving rivers. We transitioned to impenetrable jungle, over white water rivers, and tremendous lakes. It was a beautiful country and indeed lived up to its nickname of the "Pearl of Africa." As we continued south Lake Victoria came into view looking like an ocean due to its massive size. We

Figure 23.3. A flight of two CH47's arriving at Entebbe airfield. You can see the UN aircraft on the tarmac and Lake Victoria in the background. Photo by Sandra Smith.

knew we were getting close to Entebbe airport and our last stop until returning to the U.S.

The CH-47 landed on the airfield near several of the U.N. painted Russian MI-24 Hind Attack helicopters. Again I thought how odd it was to see the U.N. using the aircraft of what was once our

225

greatest adversary. We moved our equipment inside the metal hangar that served as the staging area for incoming and outgoing personnel. Upon arrival, I checked in with the USARAF team who informed me it appeared as though our contract aircraft may be delayed. I made several calls to our headquarters in the U.S. and conferred with the USARAF logistics team and was able to get approval to move the 560th team over to a local hotel. The same residence that was essentially taken over in Entebbe by the USARAF and the helicopter crews supporting Natural Fire 10. We left our boxed equipment at the hangar and moved by shuttle bus with our personal gear (rucksacks) over to Hotel Victoria to await our final lift to the U.S.

The Entebbe airport was the designated aerial port of debarkation (APOD) and was being managed by a skeleton crew of USARAF personnel. As soon as the mission ended in Kitgum a majority of the USARAF senior personnel returned to their home base in Vicenza, Italy. And why not, the operation had commenced without a hitch to that point so who would assume that the final phase would be any different. Unfortunately for the remaining USARAF personnel and the ever-growing group moving from their previous posting in Kitgum, the contract airlift began experiencing a plethora of issues in transit from the U.S. to Uganda. By this time all of the previous Task Force personnel, now numbering over 300, were essentially stuck at Entebbe in facilities that were not designed nor prepared for other than a temporary (less than 24 hour) stay.

The APOD was essentially a metal hangar and large tent. It was designed to accommodate the equipment and personnel in groups of not greater than 100 for transitional periods consisting of a few hours at a time. It was to serve as a waiting area and not a lodging facility. The weather that had been so generous to the Kitgum group now posed a problem in Entebbe with rains flooding the tented areas where a majority of the troops were staying. Despite the availability of a hotel that was being used throughout the operation by the USARAF staff, the majority of the forces were not approved

Figure 23.4. Heavy rains hit the APOD and flooded the limited accomodations creating a challenging leadership situation for the units in transit to the U.S. Photo by Sandra Smith.

to stay in the facility due to funding constraints. Now there were real problems facing the leadership including providing accommodations, feeding several hundred people for an unknown duration, and the morale of the personnel.

Because the USARAF leadership team departed so quickly there was a void in solving this new set of problems. In typical management fashion, the staffers tried desperately to figure out a way to refine the outgoing process despite the fact that that process was immaterial at this point. Even within our team I sensed a problem with unmet expectations. At the beginning of our stay in Entebbe, the initial location at Hotel Victoria seemed more than adequate to stay a day or so. However, as each day passed there was an undercurrent of disappointment and I had to get the team together and give them the *once over* regarding their morale and the situation. In essence, I imparted that: (1) we had been given a gift of a few days in Entebbe so use it to explore and learn something more about Uganda – you probably will not get another opportunity like this, (2) The aircraft situation was out of our control so you shouldn't get upset or disgruntled – there was nothing you can do to fix the aircraft, and (3) We were still considered the senior element and needed to role model for everyone else – that meant staying upbeat about the situation.

A key construct during this period was to develop and communicate new expectancies regarding this final phase of the mission. Remember from the tenets of expectancy theory that meeting people's expectations does not guarantee satisfaction while not meeting expectations does guarantee dissatisfaction. What the collective leadership teams were facing within their ranks were the continued unmet expectations regarding travel, simple accommodations, freedom of movement, food service, and situational understanding.

With the USARAF group somewhat stalled in its decision-making and prioritization, the 560th BFSB leadership attempted to fill the void despite having reverted back to its initial configuration. We began attending each of the staff meetings and applying our team members to assist in developing a number of initiatives to alleviate the suffering at the Entebbe. For the 560th personnel, the focus on something other than their own situation proved extremely useful for directing their attention on things they could improve. The simple actions of providing routine information briefings regarding the aircraft situation, opening rooms at the hotel for people to take a shower and perform some general personnel hygiene, providing a pass system to allow people to visit locations in Entebbe, and a shuttle service to bring those at their airport to the hotel for food service proved instrumental for developing a positive environment from what was turning into a very negative situation.

Ultimately, the contract aircraft resolved their maintenance problems and arrived at Entebbe. However, the last three days were a real challenge for unit leaders during Natural Fire 10. It was a somber reminder that you must stay engaged during recovery operations and not assume a "mission accomplished" perspective. Leaving the responsibility to others for safe passage back to your home base is a recipe for dysfunction. It is easy for unmet expectations to lead to dissatisfaction. Directing people on what they can accomplish instead of what they cannot control is a good method for creating positive energy instead of combatting negativity. The systems we put in place at Entebbe worked to mitigate the negative situation that sought to undermine the positive aspects of the mission close in Kit-gum. No issues surfaced from the pass system and people were able to experience another aspect of Uganda instead of being cooped up in the flooded hangar. The lesson for leaders is to recognize that closing times are transitional periods that if left un-led, can ruin a great operation.

CHAPTER TWENTY FOUR

Results

The final results of Task Force Kitgum during Natural Fire 10 were impressive and included 11,698 persons treated through the medical and dental capacity building events. Three facilities (two schools and one health center) were renovated and 636 soldiers from five African countries trained in a variety of disaster response measures. The Task Force conducted seven radio broadcasts, and numerous outreach events to communicate with the citizenry. A successful logistics and forward staging operation was established in a remote site with hundreds of safe flight hours flown and miles driven without incidence. All these activities directed by an integrated multinational TOC that synchronized, resourced and tracked the 1,009 U.S. and East African personnel who accomplished the mission. Amazingly during Natural Fire 10, the Task Force sustained only two injuries, had no violations of local law, reported no equipment lost or damaged, and all of the coalition units returned to their host countries safely (VanAmburgh, 2011).

Some of the lessons gleaned from this mission and imparted on the members were included the use of integration (at all echelons) as an organizing principle to achieve unity of effort; the importance of deliberate relationship building activities and their ability to sustain the mission; the value of engagement to engender popular support ingenuity and continuous attention; and the knowledge that performing humanitarian and disaster relief is a challenge but building the capacity of others to help people in need is a tremendous reward (VanAmburgh, 2011).

Figure 24.1. The cultural day began with some good natured competition among the coalition members. Here African soldiers and a Marine compete in a multi-sport event. Photo by Sandra Smith.

On one of the final days of Natural Fire 10 a cultural event was scheduled. The purpose was to conclude this important mission with some good-natured competition and celebration. All of the activities centered round the red clay parade field. Tents were erected to shade personnel from the sun, food was brought in from Kitgum, and fields of play were marked off. The day began with tournament of events designed to pitch each of the multinational platoons against one another in one last opportunity to determine the highest performing group. Following the competitive events was an "exhibition" between the countries for demonstration of their local dance. This put the American personnel in a predicament because we could not really determine what dance the U.S. was noteworthy for. Was it the square-dance, the electric slide, or dirty dancing? No one could identify a signature dance and we had an "out" and took it, leaving it to our coalition partners to dance and sing.

In the afternoon for additional entertainment and cultural awareness a troop of local Ugandan dancers were scheduled to perform on the basecamp. Additionally an all-day local market was set-up along the periphery of the parade field to allow the Task Force personnel an opportunity to leave there money behind before they departed – as I had promised to the Kitgum Mayor. For many of the vendors and local citizens this opportunity for commerce and cultural exchange between the Task Force participants and local residents represented a huge opportunity. People walked for several days for the chance to meet the Task Force members and for some to sell their wares in the makeshift market.

It was an awesome day. The competition further drew the Task Force together and we presented awards to recognize the top performing athletes and integrated teams. The coalition dance exhibition was a comical event bringing laughter to everyone present including the many local cit-

Figure 24.2. Formal dancing troup performing at the Cultural Day. Photo by Sandra Smith.

izens now sharing in the activities on the basecamp. Wherever you looked, you were witness to an inspiring scene of oneness. By the end of the formal dancing program it appeared like a gathering of an extended family, albeit an eclectic family. The camaraderie was more than we had hoped for our Task Force early in the planning phase, not only were the military units acting as one but the crowd was completely integrated. It looked as though every U.S. serviceperson had a Ugandan child on his or her lap. The mixture of various camouflage uniforms with the bright colored clothes of the local residents made for tapestry of color. Smiles and laughter were in abundant supply and many people were singing and dancing together to the chant of a local beat. Then the rain came – a tremendous and sudden downpour (VanAmburgh, 2011).

I remember thinking this will not be a good closer for a great day. Unbeknownst to me, and most of the Task Force members coming to the same conclusion, rain occurrences during dancing is considered good luck among the Acholi people. So while we were thinking about the potentially negative consequences of the rain, the actual response was just the opposite of what one might have guessed. People began dancing even wilder and singing louder. At one point, the downpour hit even harder and people danced even more jubilantly splashing mud and singing joyfully. It was if the rain was a sort of validation of the interactions, cooperation and relationships formed over the mission. It was at that moment when a local Ugandan woman dancing in the crowd, soaked with rain and covered with mud, tears of joy in her eyes, grabbed the Task Force CSM, hugged his face and cried "This is the best day of my life."

Our coalition presence and this event provided a legacy of healing and hope for better days in Kitgum. Think for a moment about baby Cage. At some point in the future when Cage gets older and is asked how he was named, he has a story to tell. "The Americans were here. An American delivered me. And, they put a roof on this school and they helped us renovate this medical clinic. And, oh-by-the-way the Kenyans, Rwandans, Tanzanians and Burundians were all working here together to help us." That is quite a legacy.

Natural Fire 10 served as an example of cooperation, relationship building and teamwork in this difficult region. The Ugandans, like the overjoyed Ugandan woman, suffered incredible hardships during the previous 15 years including famine, epidemic disease, civil war and incredible brutality perpetuated by insurgents. Despite their situation, many of these people walked for several days to participate in the Task Force festivities. They did so to interact, if just for a few moments, with a team of U.S. and East Africans partners who came to provide some comfort, support and hope for a better future. It was a marvel to be part of a force and community that truly unified for a higher purpose. We all learned a great deal from our experience and I believe that the Ugandan woman's display of emotion summed it up for us all.

Appendix
Leadership Strategies

This appendix is designed as a quick reference guide for leaders. Each of the five sections of the book is identified by bold text. The corresponding strategy and key lessons have been condensed to concise statements for ease of use. Your personal preparation to lead, including employment of the strategies contained herein, will greatly enhance your ability to direct complex endeavors both small and large.

Table A.1

Strategies for Leading

SECTION 1	STRATEGIES	KEY LESSONS
Leadership Pages 13-50	Learn to Lead	Be the first to "step off."
		There is no single leader solution for all variables.
		Each of the main leadership approaches have value: trait, behavioral, situational/contingency, power and influence, and transformational.
	Role-model Positive Behaviors	Role modeling is a tremendous influencer on employee behavior.
	Be Transformational	Move your organization ahead through your people.
		A "leader's job is to make others successful."
	Employ Expectancy Theory	Exceeding expectations will not guarantee satisfaction but not achieving expectations will always guarantee dissatisfaction.
		Clarity and communications are key for meeting performance expectancies.
	Understand Commitment	Satisfaction and dissatisfaction are merely temporal impressions, focus on commitment to gauge employee attachment to your organization.
		Strive for affective commitment in your organization.

Table A.2

Strategies for Leading an Organization

SECTION 2	STRATEGIES	KEY LESSONS	
Leading an Organization Pages 51-105	Delve into Organizational Culture	Link artifacts, espoused values and underlying assumptions. Strive for an organization where the things people see, hear, and believe are congruent.	
		Word+Action=Truth. Changing underlying assumptions is hard and requires you to act.	
		Control culture or it will control you.	
	Build Your Team	Adhocracy	Recognize you will likely be working ad hoc (for this).
		Right People	Request or allocate educated, experienced, and influential members from the participating agencies.
		Group Development	Prepare for the general psychosocial dynamics of group maturation - have a plan to provide structure for the team
		Relationships	Know that relationships are paramount for success - devote time and resources to this critical element
	Prepare to Lead each Phase	Planning Phase	Authoritarian Style
		Preparation Phase	Participative Style
		Training Phase	Participative Style
		Travelling Phase	Delegative Style
		Staging Phase	Participative Style
		Conduct the Mission Phase	Delegative Style
		Recovery Phase	Authoritarian
		Returning Phase	Delegative
		Refitting Phase	Participative
	Structure Your Organization	Form follows functions.	
		Strive for integration at all levels.	

Table A.3

Leader Strategies for Building a Coalition

SECTION 3	STRATEGIES	KEY LESSONS
Building a Coalition Pages 107-150	Have some Faith	You cannot control all the variables - God is there so have hope.
	Structure Social Arrangements	Food sharing is a near universal way to build relationships. An invitation is considered a gesture of hospitality and a structured meal will often force interaction.
	Organize for Process Ownership	Process ownership gives visibility and responsibility to one individual for the entire end-to-end business process. Ensure you appoint the right owner.
	Employ Peer Influence	People and thier organizations seek legitimacy and association. Peer pressure, behavior display and structuring opportunities are very effective methods for obtaining conforming behaviors.
	Schedule Training Opportunities	Structured training focuses effort, builds common understanding among members, and supports the group maturation process. If it is worth doing, it's worth rehearsing.
	Foster Competition	Cooperative competition is helpful for improving enterprise-wide performance. Build healthy competition that fosters collaboration and brings people together.

Table A.4

Leader Strategies for Engagement and Operations

SECTION 4	STRATEGIES	KEY LESSONS
Engagement and Operations Pages 151-212	Structure Workplace Communications	Your environment should reflect your leadership philosophy and the mission goals. Whenever possible move from rows to circles. Find an unstructured location for social interaction and alternative decision-making.
	Employ PACE	Primary-Alternate-Contingency-Emergency is a good model to follow. Employ multiple means and modalities to ensure information reaches required audiences at the individual, team and higher levels.
	Listen to the People on the Ground	Be humble and expect to learn from others. Assume you do not have all the information. The best information is often from the person closest to the action.
	Make it Personal	When faced with structural or ideological barriers to dialogue, redirect and connect by making the conversation personal.
	Engage, Engage, Engage	Find the best way to communicate and build relationships in order to gain commitment. Assess, adjust, and keep messages flowing and feedback open.
	Get Out There	Management by walkig around opens dialogue, provides reassurance and checks morale. The higher your stature or rank, the more effort it takes to go out and connect with people. If you are spending too much time in your office - you're wrong.
	Let Your People Go	Empower using the dimensions of potency, meaningfulness, autonomy and impact. Operationalize empowerment by trust, resources and accountability. If you allow your people to do good works, they will. Capture the stories and reward success.

Table A.5

Leader Strategies for Closing Operations

SECTION 5	STRATEGIES	KEY LESSONS
Mission **Complete** Pages 213-234	Live Continuous Improvement	Make continuous improvement a part of everything you are doing. "If you are not getting better, then you must be getting worse." Never stay satisfied with the status quo and remember: as soon as you think you've got this, you are done. Do your best to capture and document the lessons you learn for others.
	Stay Focused to the End	People have the tendency to look toward home at the end of a mission. Transitions are often the most dangerous periods in an operation. Be involved and fully engaged to combat complacency.
	Measure and Celebrate Results	Collect data for measuring success. Recognize true value is found when human potential is realized serving others. Reiterate to your team how they accomplished the mission. Celebrate the important things.

References

Army Doctrine & Training Publication, 6-22. (2012). *Army Leadership*. Washington, DC: Department of the Army. 1.

Ashmos, D.P., & Nathan, M.L. (2002). Team sense-making: a mental model for navigating uncharted territories. *Journal of Managerial Issues*. Retrieved on Dec 29, 2008 from ABI/INFORM.

Bass, B. (2005). *Transformational Leadership, 2nd ed*. New York: Psychology Press.

Bass, B. (1990). *Bass and Stogdill's Handbook of Leadership: Theory, Research and Managerial Applications (3rd ed.)*. New York: Free Press.

Becker, T., & Billings, R. (1993). Profiles of commitment: An empirical test. *Journal of Organizational Behavior, 14*. 177-190.

Beers, P.J., Boshuizen, H. P, Kirschner, P.A., & Gijselears, W. H. (2006). Common ground, complex problems and decision making. *Group Decision and Negotiation, 15*. Retrieved from Dec 29, 2008, from EBSCO.

Blake, R.., & Mouton, J. (1985). *The Managerial Grid III: The Key to Leadership Excellence*. Houston: Gulf Publishing Co.

Breen, V., Fetzer, R., Howard, L., & Preziosi, R. (2005, December). Consensus problem-solving increases perceived communication openness in organizations. *Employee Responsibilities and Rights Journal, 4*. Retrieved on Dec 29, 2008, from EBSCO.

Brown, B., Bakken, J., Ameringer, S., & Mahon, S. (2008). A comprehensive conceptualization of the peer influence process in adolescence. In M. Prinstein & K. Dodge, eds. *Understanding Peer Influence in Adolescents*. New York: Guilford Press. 17-27.

Central Intelligence Agency. (n.d.). *Uganda Map.* Retrieved online from: https://www.cia.gov/library/publications/the-world-factbook/graphics/maps/ug-map.gif

Chiaramonte, P., & Adria, M. (1994). *Face to Face: Interpersonal Communication in the Workplace.* Ontario: Prentice Hall.

Dallaire, R. (2003). *Shake hands with the devil: The failure of Humanity in Rwanda.* New York: Carroll & Graf.

Daniels, T., & Spiker, B. (1991). *Perspectives on Organizational Communication, 2ⁿᵈ ed.* Iowa: Brown Publishers. 39-40.

Deephouse, D., & Suchman, M. (2008). Legitimacy in organizational institutionalism. In R. Greenwood, C. Oliver, K. Sahlin-Anderson, & R. Suddaby, eds. *Handbook of Organizational Institutionalism.* London: Sage. 49-77.

Enlow, J.G. (2003). *Food sharing past and present: archeological evidence for economic and social interactions.* Retrieved online at http:www.uiowa.edu/~zooarch/bf20031%201%20article.pdf

Feinman, S. (1979). An evolutionary theory of food sharing. *Social Science Infomormation, 18.* 695-726.

Fellowship. [Def_]. (n.d.). *Online Etymology Dictionary.* Retrieved February 1, 2014, from http://www.etyonline.com/index.php?term=fellowship

Flournoy, M. A. (2008, January 29). *Achieving Unity of Effort in Interagency Operations.* Prepared statement for House Armed Services Subcommittee on Oversight and Investigations: Hearing on Prospects for Effective Interagency Collaboration on National Security. Washington, DC: Center for a New American Security.

French, J., & Raven, B. (1959). The bases of social power. In W. Natemeyer & J. Gilberg eds. (1989). *Classics of Organizational Behavior, 2ⁿᵈ ed.* Illinois: Interstate Printers and Publishers.

Gibbons, T., Hurley, D., & Moore, S. (1998, Winter). Interagency operations centers: An opportunity we cannot ignore. *Parameters.* Retrieved 14 Feb 2009 at smallwarsjournal.com/documents/iaoperationscenters.pdf

Henderson-Loney, J. (1996). Tuckman and tears: developing teams during profound organizational change. *Supervision, 5.* Retrieved on Dec 29, 2008 from ABI/INFORM.

Hersey, P. & Blanchard, K. (1988). *Management of Organization Behavior: Utilizing Human Resources.* New Jersey: Prentice-Hall.

Hofstede, G. (1980, Summer). Motivation, leadership and organization: do American theories apply abroad? *Organizational Dynamics.* Retrieved on Dec 29, 2008, from EBSCO.

Hollen, P., Mundell, T., Nilson, D., & Sweeney, M. (2003). *Pre-planning and Post-conflict CMOC/CIMIC Challenges.* Retrieved online from www.jfsc.ndu/current_students/documents_policies/documents/jca_cca_awsp/Pre-Planning_and_Post-Conflict.doc

Howitt A., & Leonard, H. (2009). *Managing Crises: Responses to Large-scale Emergencies.* Washington, DC: CQ Press.

JCSE. (2014). *Joint communications support element.* Retrieved from http://www.jecc.mil/SubordinateCommands/JointCommunicationsSupportElement.aspx

Joint Publication 3.0. (2011). *Joint Operations.* Washington, DC: Government Printing Office.

Joint Publication 3-16 (2013). *Multinational Operations.* Washington, DC: U.S. Government Printing Office.

Joint Publication 5-0 (2006). *Joint Operation Planning.* Washington, DC: U.S. Government Printing Office.

Kaplan, H., & Gurven, M. (2001). *The Natural History of Human Food Sharing and Cooperation: A Review of a New Multi-individual Approach to Negotiation of Norms.* Retrieved February 1, 2014, from http://www.

Kirkman, B., & Rosen, B. (1999). Antecedents and consequences of team empowerment. *Academy of Management Journal, 42.* 58-74. Retrieved March 14, 2015 from http://www.jstor.org/stable/256874

Kobasa, S., Maddi, S., & Kahn, S. (1982). Hardiness and health: A prospective study. *Journal of Personality and Social Psychology, 42.* 168-177.

Legitimacy [Def. _] (n.d.). *Online Etymology Dictionary.* Retrieved February 1, 2014, from http://www.etyonline.com/index. php?term=legitimate

Luck, G., & Findlay, M. (2008, July). *Joint Operations Insights and Best Practices, 2nd Ed.* Norfolk, VA: U.S. Joint Forces Command.

Medina, F.J., Lourdes, M., Dorado, M.A., Martinez, I.,& Guerra, J.M. (2005). Types of intragroup conflict and affective reactions. *Journal of Managerial Psychology, 3/4.* Retrieved on Dec 29, 2008 from ABI/INFORM.

Meyer, J., & Allen, N. (1991). A three-component conceptualization of organizational commitment. *Human Resource Management review, I.* 61-89.

Meyer J., Allen, N., & Smith, C. (1993). Commitment to organizations and occupations: Extenstion and test of a three-component conceptuatlization. *Journal of Applied Psychology,* 17, 538-551.

Meyer, J., & Allen, N. (1997). *Commitment on the Workplace: Theory, Research and Application.* California: Sage.

Mintzberg, H., & Mchugh, A. (1985). Strategy formation in adhocracy. *Administrative Science Quarterly, 30.* Retrieved online.

Montebello, A.R., & Buzzotta, V. R. (1993). Work teams that work. *Training and Development, 3.* Retrieved on Dec 29, 2008 from ABI/INFORM.

Northouse, P. (1997). *Leadership Theory and Practice.* Thousand Oaks, CA: Sage.

Onions, C. (Ed.). (1996). The OxfordDictionary of English Etymology. Oxford: Clarendon Press.

Peelle, H.E. (2006, December). Appreciative inquiry and creative problem solving in cross functional teams. *Journal of Applied Behavioral Science, 4.* Retrieved on Dec 29, 2008 from ABI/IN-

FORM.

Peters, T., & Waterman, R. (1982). *In Search of Excellence: Lessons from America's Best-Run Companies.* Harper-Collins.

Prinstein & Dodge (2008). *Understanding Peer Influence in Adolescents.* New York: Guilford Press.

Quick, J.C., Quick, J. D., Nelson, D.L., & Hurrell, J.J. (1997). *Preventative Stress Management in Organizations.* Washington, DC: American Psychological Association.

Rasmussen, L. B. (2003).The facilitation of groups and networks: capabilities to shape creative cooperation. *AI and Society, 17.* Retrieved on Dec 29, 2008 from EBSCO.

Schein, E. (2004). *Organizational Culture and Leadership, 3 ed.* San Francisco, CA: Jossey-Bass.

Suchman, M.C. (1995). Managing legitimacy: Strategic and institutional approaches. *Academy of Management Review.* 20/3. 571-610.

Tuckman, B.W., & Jensen, M.A (1977, December). Stages of small-group development revisited. *Group and Organizational Studies, 4.* Retrieved on Dec 29, 2008 from ABI/INFORM.

United Nations (2006). *Draft outline for Post Conflict Needs Assessment Review: Liberia.* Retrieved on Feb 14, 2009 at www.undg.org/archive docs/8886-Liberia PCNA Case Study.doc.

VanAmburgh, P. (2011, May-June). One mission to Africa: Lessons for a lifetime. *Journal of International Peace Operations, 6,6.* 11-12.

Vroom, V. (1964). *Work and Motivation.* New York: Wiley.

Yeatts, D., & Hyten, C. (1998). *High Performing Self-Managed Work Teams: Comparison of Theory to Practice.* Thousand Oaks, CA: Sage.

Yeh, Y.J., & Chou, H.W. (2005). Team composition and learning behaviors in cross functional teams. *Social Behavior and Personality, 33.* Retrieved on Dec 29, 2008 from EBSCO.

Subject Index

Glossary of Military Acronyms

AAR	After Action Review
AFRICOM	African Command
APOD	Aerial Port of Debarkation
BFSB	Battlefield Surveillance Brigade
C3	Command, Control and Communications
CA	Civil Affairs
CASEVAC	Casualty Evacuation
CENTCOM	Central Command
CJTF	Coalition Joint Task Force
CSM	Command Sergeant Major
DCO	Defense Connect Online
EUCOM	European Command
EVD	Ebola Virus Disease
FOB	Forward Operating Base
FTX	Field Training Exercise
HALO	High Altitude Low Opening
HCA	Humanitarian and Civic Assistance
HF	High Frequency
HMMWV	High Mobility Multi-Wheel Vehicle
IDF	Israeli Defense Force
IED	Improvised Explosive Device
IO	Information Operations
JCSE	Joint Communications Support Element
JTF	Joint Task Force
LRA	Lord's Resistant Army
LRS	Long Range Surveillance

LZ	Landing Zone
MRE	Meal Ready to Eat
NCO	Noncommissioned Officer
NGO	Non-governmental Organization
NORTHCOM	Northern Command
ODA	Operational Detachment Alpha
PA	Public Affairs
PACE	Primary Alternate Contingency Emergency
PACOM	Pacific Command
PSYOPS	Psychological Operations
QRF	Quick Reaction Force
RSOI	Reception Staging Onward Integration
S1	Administration
S2	Intelligence
S3	Operations
S4	Logistics
SAW	Squad Automatic Weapon
S/C	Single Channel
SINCGARS	Single Channel Ground and Airborne Radio System
SOCOM	Special Operations Command
SOUTHCOM	Southern Command
TACSAT	Tactical Satellite
TOC	Tactical Operations Center
TTP	Tactics, Techniques and Procedures
UN	United Nations
UPDF	Ugandan People's Defense Force
USARAF	U.S. Army Africa
USMC	U.S. Marine Corps
VIP	Very Important Person
VOIP	Voice Over Internet Protocol
XO	Executive Officer

About the Author

Peter VanAmburgh received a Doctor of Education in Organizational Leadership from Argosy University in 2003. He is the President of 1Mission Leadership LLC, a consulting, education and training company located in northen suburbs of Atlanta, GA. In 2012 he retired from the U.S. Army as a Colonel after 28 years of demanding leadership roles from company/team through brigade command in Long Range Surveillance, Special Forces, and Intelligence units. He holds master's degrees from Kennesaw State University and the U.S. Army War College, and is a graduate of a host of military schools including Special Forces, Ranger, Jumpmaster, HALO, Pathfinder, and the Counterintelligence Special Agent course. He has the benefit of possessing unique technical competencies as well as experience leading large organizations and highly skilled multinational teams in combat operations, humanitarian missions, and other activities in over 15 countries around the world. In addition to his military service, he has three years of law enforcement, five years in business, and over six years of teaching experience at undergraduate through doctoral level.

Dr. VanAmburgh values integrity, loyalty, service and action. His work bridges the strategic to the tactical and his teaching is as valuable for senior executives as to their first line supervisors. He is a master at strategic planning, deciphering culture, and developing action plans that deliver results. He is also a lifelong learner who lives his favorite mantra, "If you are not getting better – you must be getting worse." His passion is passing on the hard-learned lessons from the battlefield, boardroom, classroom, and the street, to the next generation of global leaders.

Made in the USA
Columbia, SC
14 April 2018